HOME AND CONDO DEFECTS:

A CONSUMER GUIDE TO FAULTY CONSTRUCTION

Thomas E. Miller
and
Rachel M. Miller

SEVEN LOCKS PRESS

Santa Ana, California
Minneapolis, Minnesota
Washington, D.C.

Seven Locks Press
P.O. Box 25689
Santa Ana, CA 92799
(800) 354-5348

Individual Sales. This book is available through most bookstores or can be ordered directly from Seven Locks Press at the address above.

Quantity Sales. Special discounts are available on quantity purchases by corporations, associations, and others. For details, contact the "Special Sales Department" at the publisher's address above.

Printed in the United States of America

Library of Congress Cataloging-in-Publication Data
is available from the publisher
ISBN 0-929765-83-4

Cover and Interior Design by Sparrow Advertising & Design
Illustrations by: Building Analysts, San Diego, California, 800-352-1497

The Miller Law Firm
800-403-3332
www.constructiondefects.com

TABLE OF CONTENTS

Why We Think You Need This Handbook

After practicing in the area of construction defect litigation for nearly three decades, we have come to realize that little information is available to aid homeowners in determining whether construction defects exist in their houses and even less on what to do if defects do exist.

Although we have written extensively for lawyers and other professionals about construction defect litigation, we have attempted only a few short pamphlets for consumers. This book is an outgrowth of one of these pamphlets, *What To Do If Your House or Condo Is Defective*, which consists of twelve common questions and answers about construction defects. This pamphlet is in Appendix C.

This book is designed to aid the consumer who believes he or she may have a construction defect in his or her home, or the consumer who is involved in a construction defect claim. We want to explain a complex legal area so that you, the consumer, can gain a basic understanding of it.

Construction defect claims continue to rise as the population and new home construction increase. The 1990 United States Census results shows that the western region leads all others in growth rates, with Nevada showing an incredible 31.9 percent population increase, followed closely by Utah and Arizona.

As defect claims have grown and the law has become more complex, lawyers have had to expand their areas of expertise while still being able to explain to their clients, in layman's terms, what happens in a construction defect lawsuit. The successful construction defect lawyer must be a skillful trial attorney and have a working knowledge of many other fields involved in these claims—such as civil engineering, geology, structural engineering, and construction techniques—and an understanding of new ways of solving consumer problems without necessarily making use of the court system.

It is impossible to refer to each law as it applies in the various states. Instead, we have attempted to summarize the law so our non-lawyer readers will have a general understanding of it. To accomplish this, occasionally we repeat information where there is overlap among the issues.

Please note that the purpose of this book is not to provide legal advice or direction. Our sole intention is to educate consumers by providing pertinent information about what to look for and how to work with your lawyer in a construction defect case. If you believe you have a construction defect problem, you should contact a competent attorney before acting. If you have any questions or comments, we can be reached online at <u>Info@constructiondefects.com</u> or by mail using the tear-out form on the inside book cover.

ACKNOWLEDGEMENTS

We are grateful for the contributions of many people whose efforts made this handbook possible. The past and present attorneys, paralegals, staff, and consultants to the Miller Law Firm and its predecessor, The Law Offices of Thomas E. Miller, are to be recognized at the outset for meeting the demands of their busy schedules while providing assistance during the preparation of this work.

ABOUT THE AUTHORS

Thomas E. Miller is the founder and president of the Miller Law Firm, representing homeowners and associations throughout the United States. Mr. Miller has recovered more than $350 million dollars on behalf of homeowners and associations. Mr. Miller received his B.A. from California State University, Long Beach, and his J.D. from the University of California, Hastings College of Law. A nationally recognized specialist on construction defect and land subsidence claims, Mr. Miller has written and lectured extensively on these subjects. He is the author of three legal textbooks on construction defects, his most recent is *Handling Construction Defect Claims - Western States Third Edition* (Aspen Law & Business 1999), numerous publications including Construction Defect Handbook for the Board of Directors and Property Managers, and many articles in the field. He has been the principal speaker at university extension programs, tailored to educate community association managers and board members, at the University of California, Irvine; California State University, Long Beach; and the University of Nevada at Las Vegas. Mr. Miller has been a featured speaker with such trade and industry groups as the Community Associations Institute (CAI), the California Association of Community Managers (CACM), the Institute of Real Estate Management, and Executive Council of Homeowners. He has been featured media expert on construction defects with such national newspapers as *The New York Times, Los Angeles Times, Orange County Register, San Francisco Chronicle, Las Vegas Sun, The Oregonian, The Arizona Republic, Los Angeles Daily Journal, National Geographic,* and *The National Law Journal.* A member of the State Bars of California and Colorado, Mr. Miller is also a member of the California, Nevada, Arizona,

Oregon, and Florida Trial Lawyers Associations, American Bar Association, American Arbitration Association, and numerous local bar associations. Currently serving on the Board of Directors of the Consumer Attorneys of California, he is an active member of CAI and a founding member of CACM. Mr. Miller frequently associates with attorneys and law firms in other states to pursue construction defect claims on behalf of homeowners.

Rachel M. Miller is the co-author of *Handling Construction Defect Claims-Western States Third Edition* and is marketing partner of the Miller Law Firm. She received her B.A. from Loyola Marymount University in Los Angeles, and her J.D. from California Western School of Law in San Diego. In her unique role in the Miller Law firm, Ms. Miller has been featured in *The Los Angeles Times, Orange County Register,* and *San Diego Daily Commerce,* as well as on numerous television and radio programs. Ms. Miller is a founding member of the California Association of Community Managers (CACM) and regularly speaks to the community association industry and law firm practice forums. She has also authored and lectured extensively in community association and legal forums on consumer legislation, disaster response, construction defects, media relations, and marketing. To further her involvement in the community association industry, she is a member of thirteen chapters of the Community Associations Institute (CAI), a member of the elite President's Club, a founding member of the CACM, the Executives of Homeowner Organizations, and the Institute of Real Estate Management. Ms. Miller has served on numerous committees and boards of these organizations, and has been honored with numerous awards from them. She has been the editor, coordinator, and moderator of university extension programs on construction defect law for community associations, including courses at the University of California, Irvine; California State University, Long Beach; and University of Nevada, Las Vegas. Ms. Miller is a member of the California State Bar, Consumer Attorneys of California Board of Directors, Legal Marketing Associaton and the Orange County Bar Association.

INTRODUCTION

With housing units popping up like wildflowers on what seems like every piece of open space available on hillsides, in valleys, on earthquake faults, and even on toxic waste sites, construction defect problems are growing at an equally fast pace. The law, of course, is attempting to keep up with a changing building environment and with consumers' changing needs.

As you can deduce from the following chapters, such claims require considerable work and effort by homeowners and associations. Why, then, are the claims increasing?

Part of the problem is just the sheer number of new houses being built in short time frames. The more houses built, the more mistakes can be made. Another part of the problem is that in many communities the land most suited for housing already has been used. Builders are left with the complex problem of carving out hillsides and filling in valleys so they can build homes. Doing it right requires care. Instead builders frequently cut corners to save a few dollars and increase profits.

Shoddy workmanship is another reason claims are increasing. Because housing is mass-produced, old skills practiced by trained craftsmen who built individually constructed homes are being lost. To increase speed and profit, the mass-production housing industry sometimes slaps housing together without paying attention to detail and precision. Builders use cheaper materials, not to save money for the consumer but to increase profits for themselves.

For example, after World War II, when millions of returning veterans began buying mass-produced housing, many builders started using galvanized piping (or worse) for plumbing, and aluminum wiring for electrical systems. Both corroded, and the aluminum wiring even caused homes to burn down. Builders failed to reinforce slabs with sufficient steel. They failed to double-check the soil to be sure it would support a house and not shift, buckle, or erode away. One builder even ran galvanized piping for natural gas through the concrete slab. The pipes rusted, leaked gas into homes, and presented potentially deadly results.

Another problem was the components that were produced offsite. No longer did a skilled carpenter carefully build a wood window frame that perfectly fit the framing. No longer did experienced masons build finely designed fireplaces. New space-age industrial external wall coverings replaced wood siding. Roofers stopped using wood shingles or slate on well-slanted roofs. Instead, they used tar components on flat roofs, or composite roofs covered with rocks on surfaces with too little slant. Windows and doors, along with many other items, were produced in factories miles away, often with insufficient quality control and design tolerances.

This meant less expensive housing could be built for a mass market, but quality was sacrificed for quantity. The result was that many states decided to apply strict liability legal concepts—similar to those applied to other mass-produced products, such as automobiles or table saws—to construction defect actions. Other states increased the use of older remedies such as negligence, implied warranties, fraud, and breach of contract. And let's face facts: Because of strict liability and similar claims houses are better built today, just as automobiles are safer and last longer.

An additional source of problems was the rise in common interest housing. To obtain government approval, developers frequently built roadways, which were owned by the residents, and decreased public expense. Generally, the homeowner association owns this common interest area, along with amenities such as hot tubs, play areas, swimming pools, tennis courts, and gyms. This means that for defects in these areas, the homeowner association itself can bring suit. In condominiums, the association frequently owns everything except the interior space and fixtures of individual apartment-style units.

The building industry complains that construction defect actions increase the cost of housing. If anything, however, the claims have benefited both the consumer and the industry.

Consumers benefit because developers, fearful of defect claims, build better and longer lasting housing. Builders pay more attention to soils tests, roofing techniques, materials selection, and other factors, which increases housing quality without significantly increasing cost. When builders fail to build to a higher standard, there are remedies available so consumers can get what they paid for.

Construction defect law saves the builders time, effort, and even money in the long run. For example, one builder used regular nails instead of galvanized roofing nails to save a few pennies per nail. When the nails corroded, the roofs leaked, the sub-roofing and framing began to rot, and the developer ended up paying millions of dollars to replace all the roofs in the development. You know that in the next project, the builder spent those few extra pennies and saved himself millions of dollars. The builder also paid stricter attention to those details in future projects, which helped him sell his product faster and rebuild his reputation for quality projects. Undoubtedly, other builders heard of the problem and made their products better, which improved their reputations and enabled them to sell their products quickly as well.

Governments kept pace by raising building standards, requiring more complete building inspections by better-trained inspectors, and setting up a more effective pre-construction approval process. This also created a more consumer-friendly environment and helped increase both housing availability and quality.

Construction defect claims also helped spot health problems within housing. "Sick building syndrome" caused people to suffer a variety of conditions from mild allergic reactions to chronic and debilitating illnesses. As a result of construction defect claims , builders more carefully built homes so there were fewer mold, mildew, rot, chemical contamination, and related problems, thus beginning the eradication of "sick building syndrome."

Of course, we have all heard of New York's infamous Love Canal. Homes built over hazardous waste sites, landfills, and other areas have created nearly insurmountable problems. Housing has been built over landfills (city dumps) that settled, and when the fill material rotted, it produced flammable methane gas that vented into the housing development. The gas had to be eliminated by directing it through giant torches that burned twenty-four hours a day. This, of course, hardly helped the residents' housing values to appreciate.

Often, developers knew of these problems and said nothing to the consumers, which is tantamount to fraud. Again, defect claims encouraged developers to disclose this information in order to avoid costly, reputation-damaging claims.

As you can see—and as this book, we hope, explains—construction defect claims have significantly improved American housing. We also hope the building industry will work with consumer groups to continue this trend.

CHAPTER ONE: THE BIG PICTURE

A Capsule Version of How It Works

A home probably is the largest investment most people make in a lifetime, but it is more than just an investment. To nearly everyone, home is where you raise your children, build a life, and attempt to fulfill the American Dream.

To many, the American Dream turns into a nightmare when, after years of saving for a down payment, you discover your new home is filled with defects, from leaky roofs, cracked walls and foundations, and flooding, to literally sliding down a hillside (so much for the view that cost thousands of dollars).

Luckily, laws governing faulty construction have evolved from the old *caveat emptor* (let the buyer beware). Today's laws include numerous ways for consumers to recover losses caused by construction defects in both residential property and commercial buildings. One recent legal development is to apply to homebuyers the consumer protections that used to apply only to automobile purchasers. It was not until 1974 that California courts ruled that homeowners had an implied warranty of "fitness for a particular use," meaning if you bought a house, you should be able to live in it comfortably while getting what you paid for, even if you are not the original buyer. Nearly all states have followed, although usually the only way to enforce your rights is with a lawyer and through the courts. This means a construction defect claim.

One construction defect claim can involve dozens of people. Today, developers, builders, contractors, subcontractors, property managers, apartment converters, lenders, architects, engineers, and other trade and professional people all can be involved in lawsuits that cover an array of legal issues.

This, of course, means that resolving a construction defect claim requires a law firm with lawyers who possess considerable legal skills, organizational skills, and the ability to aid the homeowners in finding financing for the claim. It also means that lawyers involved in construction defect cases must know their way around several very technical construction and scientific fields. They also must know who are the best experts in dozens of disciplines and be aware which expert best suits a particular situation. A law firm that limits its practice to construction defect claims should be your preferred choice.

City and other local governments have entered the fray. Because of construction defect claims, governmental entities have tightened building codes and regulations; those already existing are more stringently enforced. Local governments frequently require tract housing to make certain modifications to conform to particular geographic and geotechnical situations. For example, housing in areas subject to earthquakes may be required to modify construction to better withstand temblors. In other areas, such as California's Central Valley, water may not naturally drain. As a result, foundations retain liquids as if they are giant sponges. Therefore, special water intrusion protection and drainage systems may be required.

In other areas, the soil may consist primarily of clay. Expansion and contraction of the clay can result in cracked foundations. In those cases, building codes may require special steel reinforcements within the concrete slabs. The deserts in Arizona, Nevada, the mountains in Colorado and other states, coastal ocean bluffs, and sand dunes in Washington and Oregon may demand special building techniques. Extreme temperature variations, snowfall, or high amounts of rain may require architectural changes to standard plans to fit the environment.

What constitutes a construction defect is wide-ranging and can include environmental issues. The presence of hazardous chemicals, earthquake faults, toxic molds, termites, inadequate drainage, leaking roofs, bad plumbing, faulty wiring, cracked slabs, structural failures, electrical problems, safety code violations, defective furnaces, siding and stucco failure, failing foundations, poorly constructed sidewalks and roadways, poor soil compaction, hidden landslides and otherwise unstable soil, "sick building syndrome," and many other problems all can be considered "defects." The Americans with Disabilities Act of 1990 might be involved with claims about commercial buildings and apartments. Almost anything that can go wrong probably will go wrong, and can be a "defect."

Most homes built today belong to homeowner associations that typically own the development's roadways and other common interests. Associations and their boards of directors usually are involved in construction defect claims. Frequently, they are the ones who have the duty to retain the lawyers and bring claims that may result in legal action.

Also, homeowners themselves must be educated and guided through what can be a very complex process. The homeowner's participation is critical in pursuing a claim.

First, defects must be discovered and analyzed. Next, many states require that extensive pre-litigation statutory requirements be satisfied. If litigation is begun, homeowners will be required to devote considerable time and energy participating in what is called "discovery." This may include being questioned in depositions conducted by the opposing parties, responding to long and complex interrogatories, producing what can be hundreds of documents, and otherwise aiding the attorney preparing the case for settlement, arbitration, other forms of case resolution or, in five percent of cases, trial.

After the case is resolved, decisions regarding how the settlement is distributed and how the property is to be repaired must be made. This, in many cases, can involve dozens of homeowners, one or more homeowner associations, the management company, construction companies, and the input from many different experts. If repairs are made, the homeowner, or homeowner association, will have to supervise the efforts and will be required to help coordinate the various parties involved.

What you can recover may include monies for repairs, money for decreased home value, actual repairs, or having the developers buy back the homes. In the case of homeowner associations, this easily can total millions of dollars.

The purpose of this handbook is to help you navigate this legal quagmire. A construction defect claim could be the most difficult thing you ever do, but you have only one shot at saving your home—your largest investment—and your assets.

Chapter One Do's and Don'ts

Do:

- Do be on the lookout for defects when inspecting the property for purchase.

- Do remember defects can result from dozens of design and construction problems.

- Do retain an independent and qualified home inspector before purchasing property.

- Do read any builder warranty carefully. You'll be surprised what it does not cover.

Don't:

- Don't take the developer's word for construction quality.

- Don't be talked into a false sense of security by clever developers and brokers.

- Don't forget to notify your homeowner association of potential defects in your home.

CHAPTER TWO: JUST WHAT ARE THESE DEFECTS, ANYWAY?

Lawyers and courts seem to use different dictionaries than regular folk when it comes to home defects. Some courts have said the consumer must be able to rely on the skill of the developer to build in a "reasonably workmanlike manner," which seems to mean the builder should build it as well as it should be built. Failing to comply with this concept is referred to as "negligence." In an action for negligence, you must prove that the developers or others involved in the building process made a mistake.

This can be a difficult process. In a negligence action, the homeowner must show what the developer did wrong and, more importantly, that the developer had breached a duty and that breach caused damages. For example, suppose that because a developer used the wrong size nails a home's roof leaks. The homeowner must show that the roof leaked because the developer used the wrong sized nails, had a duty to use the correctly sized nail, and by using the wrong nails caused the roof to leak. Lawyers analyze negligence with terms like "proximate cause," "cause in fact," and what a "reasonable person" would say. In layperson's terms it all translates to: The builder goofed, everyone knows he shouldn't have goofed, and that goof caused a problem damaging the home.

Tract, or production, homes are not one-size-fits-all, and governments have responded to construction defect claims by aggressively creating more and stronger construction requirements.

The more progressive courts have said a home is defective if the builder is a "mass producer of housing and places them into the stream of commerce" (builds tract homes to be sold and eventually resold) and fails to build them as well as they should be built. This is called "strict liability," and all one must show is that there is some sort of defect.

Defects are not limited to faulty workmanship. In one case, a developer built nearly 200 homes on a beautiful bluff overlooking the Pacific Ocean. If the bluffs eroded, the homes could have fallen into the water. The courts said this was a defect and the developer was required to reinforce the bluff.

Probably the clearest definition of a construction defect comes from the Nevada courts, which say that a construction defect is a condition that materially affects, in an adverse manner, the value or use of residential property.

The Patent or Latent Controversy

Construction defects are frequently divided into two categories: They are said to be either "patent" or "latent." These are legal terms over which lawyers can spend hours fighting. The distinction is very important because it determines how much time you have for bringing suit. A patent defect is usually defined as a defect "that is apparent by reasonable inspection" by "ordinary care and prudence." For example, flooding when it rains, or failure to build a fence around a swimming pool.

A latent defect is defined as being "not apparent by reasonable inspection." For example, homebuyers cannot see rotting framing inside the walls and usually don't know about it until the house starts to fall down.

Deciding which is which should be left to your lawyer.

Is It a Defect or Did I Fail to Maintain It?

Although just about anything can be a defect, homeowners still have a responsibility to maintain their property. Developers cannot be sued because the owner didn't keep the property in good repair. For example, the owner cannot allow roof gutters to clog up with leaves and then sue because the gutters don't function properly, or, as one homeowner did, level the back yard and then blame the builder when the water didn't drain properly. Maintaining the property usually is the responsibility of either the homeowner or the homeowner association, depending on the particular situation.

Deciding whether something is the result of poor maintenance or is a defect can be a tough call. Did the gutters fail to drain because the owner failed to clear the leaves, or was it because the developer incorrectly installed the gutter system? To determine this, your lawyer probably will hire an expert who will carefully review the situation and present a conclusion.

It's a Defect, but Who is Responsible?

The developer is the first answer, but others also may be responsible. If a window leaks, the developer is responsible because he produced the house or condo. But if the window was not manufactured correctly, the manufacturer also is responsible, and perhaps it was installed incorrectly, which would make the subcontractor who installed it share responsibility.

Property managers frequently are targets of legal action. Usually, they are hired by associations to manage budgets, collect dues, care for landscaping, and perform other operational matters. If they are negligent in these tasks, or fail to recognize and investigate a potential common-area construction defect, they can be held liable.

Also, because homeowner associations and property managers hold and control homeowners' monies (and since the developer usually creates the homeowner association and sits on its board of directors), they are said to have a fiduciary duty, which is a much higher duty than simple negligence, and requires them to act responsibly. Breaching a fiduciary duty usually involves self-dealing, lack of business judgment, and conflict of interest. Also, if one shows the breach was intentional, one can receive punitive damages, which are special damages designed to punish the offender.

Breach of fiduciary duty, developer liability, and board of directors' liability can become very complex. For example, the developer has the duty after selling homes to not change construction aspects that could reduce the homebuyers' investments in later development phases.

Additional potential defendants are building inspectors and other governmental entities and agents. The historic rule is that governments are immune from lawsuits. That tradition has been slowly chipped away. However, when it comes to governmental liability, there are various technicalities and requirements, depending upon the type of government (federal, state, or local). In the case of state and local governments, the requirements vary with each particular state and locality.

A construction defect attorney must be aware that various jurisdictions have different codes, regulations, and statutes. He also must have the staff and other facilities to properly research these variations.

Whether or not a governmental entity is liable in a construction defect case depends on many factors. Among them are the laws in your particular jurisdiction: whether government action is required by law or is discretionary, the standard of care required of building inspectors or approval agencies, and whether the government committed fraud or misrepresentation. In addition, the notice requirements and statute of limitations can be very rigid and allow very short lengths of time for filing complaints. This is why it is imperative that you contact an attorney as soon as you think your property might have a construction defect.

Law schools teach entire courses on governmental liability. What you, the consumer, need to know is that time is of the essence, that government entities are potential defendants, and that all governmental reports and other information in your possession should be given to your attorney.

Chapter Two Do's and Don'ts

Do:

- Do have your lawyer explain to you in simple and clear terms the type and nature of any defect.

- Do notify your lawyer and homeowner association of any suspected defect. What appears at first to be a minor problem could develop into a catastrophic one.

- Do remember that not all defects can be easily seen. Some are hidden behind walls and under slabs.

- Do carefully maintain your property. Perform an annual checkup.

- Do remember that many people and entities are potential defendants. Don't release anyone without consulting an attorney.

Don't:

- Don't assume that just because a defect can't be seen that one does not exist. For example, excessive creaking, mold, or unpleasant odors can be signs of defects.

- Don't attempt to analyze potential defects. That is your lawyer's and expert's job.

- Don't hesitate to inform your lawyer or homeowner association of potential defects. Because of complex statutes of limitations, if you snooze, you could lose.

CHAPTER THREE:
THE INVESTIGATION

Once defects are suspected, experts (usually called consultants at this stage, but the terms are used interchangeably) are hired. They should be hired through your lawyer. If you hire them directly instead of through your attorney, their investigation results may have to be given to the developer, and you might trigger various statutes of limitations, which could destroy your case.

Your expert's job is to discover what your defects are and what is causing them. This can take time and can be expensive. The first thing your expert probably will do is walk through the development to discover and record potential defects.

This can be an expensive and time-consuming process. Experienced construction defect law firms and lawyers usually have developed specialized techniques allowing them to discover information as efficiently as possible. A law firm should have a well-developed working relationship with most of the experts involved in a defect claim, and should know which experts perform best in particular situations. Not all experts are created equal, and even experts in the same field will have differing sub-areas of expertise within that field. For example, one geotechnical expert may be more experienced in analyzing earthquake problems than another expert who works better in the area of landslides or slope movement. Some roofing experts are more experienced in discussing large, flat apartment-style roofs while another may be better with sloped roofs on individual single-family homes. Some stucco experts are better equipped to evaluate EIFS (single coat system) failures than the traditional three-coat application.

To cut costs and save time (both of which are important goals), in multi-unit developments experts frequently send survey forms originated in your attorney's office to owners and residents. In addition, your experts and attorney will examine numerous documents, such as your board of director's minutes, developer sales and advertising materials, correspondence with other lawyers and with the developer, building inspectors' reports, and governmental filings, to help determine the existence of a defect, its nature, its cause, and its extent. After analyzing the surveys, the expert will conduct site inspections and do some intrusive testing to determine what the defects are and how extensive they are.

Who the Experts Are

For every defect, there seems to be a different expert. The experts you may require include
- Architects to look at the overall construction and design
- Structural engineers to examine load-carrying walls and other structural items
- Soils (geotechnical) engineers to report on the ground, soils, and site selection
- Roofing, decking and waterproofing experts to look for leaks
- Civil engineers to check out the site grading, gutters, sidewalks, and boundary surveys, along with roads, sewage, and water delivery
- Environmental engineers to look for toxic fumes, waste, and other dangerous environmental factors
- Indoor industrial hygienists to assess for "sick building syndrome"
- Mechanical engineers to investigate heating, ventilating, air conditioning, and plumbing
- Electrical engineers to watch for electrical and lighting defects
- Cost estimators to determine the cost to fix it all

Your case may require other experts and sub-specialists who should be retained as needed. In single-family home cases, it is economical to band together with as many owners as possible to share the costs of experts.

Attorneys often advance these costs, but you should understand that ultimately you will be responsible for them.

Your attorney should carefully explain to you your expected costs and the types of experts that most likely will be retained. Usually, the agreement is reduced to a written contract so that everyone involved will fully understand his or her rights and responsibilities. Even though expert fees may be recoverable by a prevailing party, your attorney should use reasonable care to keep these fees under control. Of course, if an expert is needed, he or she should be retained. It is better to err on the side of safety, and a competent law firm is required to know when an expert most likely will be needed. You can be sure of one thing: Your builder will hire a formidable team of experts to contest your case.

The Property Manager's Role

If the homeowner association is involved, the association's property manager often plays an important role in the litigation. This, however, usually takes more time than the management company's normal duties of collecting membership dues, maintaining the property, arranging association meetings, and otherwise managing the property. Many of these extra duties mean additional costs. Among the roles the property manager can play are:

- Identifying what is a defect and what is the result of poor maintenance
- Scrutinizing repair invoices
- Reviewing owner maintenance calls
- Protecting and directing information received about the case
- Handling experts
- Making sure the experts are dealing directly with the attorney
- Arranging and running monthly meetings to deal with owner complaints
- Dealing with repairs and maintenance requests
- Meeting with owners of affected homes
- Meeting with homeowners regarding builder's offers and options

- Holding special association meetings regarding litigation
- Educating new board members and officers about the litigation
- Conducting pre-depositions and depositions
- Providing information to homeowners about outside financing for litigation
- Handling proxy solicitations for loans
- Attending settlement conferences and other required meetings
- Taking calls from buyers, escrow companies, brokers, and agents
- Making sure deed updates are current with litigation
- Monitoring special maintenance procedures during litigation
- Accounting for additional time needed to deal with experts and other lawsuit-related matters
- Managing loan payments and cash flow problems
- Interviewing reconstruction contractors and working with them
- Helping to relocate owners to temporary housing during needed repairs
- Setting repair schedules
- Setting up investment counselor interviews

Depending on the association and its contract with the management company, these duties probably will exceed normal management costs. The board of directors should be prepared to pay for these extra services. You can limit many of these costs if you choose your construction defect attorney from a law firm that has the staff and experience to perform the additional tasks otherwise left to the management company.

Usually, the developer initially retains an association's management company. Once the homeowner association is dominated by homeowners, it is probably a good idea for the board of directors to approach the management company, especially if construction defect problems are evident. The board of directors should be sure that the management company has experience in working with homeowner associations involved in claims against developers and understands that the management company is aware of the nature and extent of its responsibilities.

Types of Defects

Lawyers and experts frequently use very technical words to define defects. Most are understandable to the layperson, but many are not. Be on the lookout for the following terms:

- **Improper site selection and failure to follow soils engineering analysis.** This can mean building on an earthquake fault, on an unstable hill, a landslide, weak soils, and other site-related issues.
- **Improper landfill operations and poor compaction testing.** This usually means the property was built on soil that will sink, expand, contract, or shift.
- **Improper landscaping and irrigation.** This generally refers to flooding caused by weather or watering.
- **Improper drainage.** This generally refers to flooding caused by weather or watering.
- **Design defects.** This includes faulty mechanical or utility systems such as furnaces, air conditioning, and water heaters.
- **Poor materials selection and faulty construction techniques.** This means leaky roofs (probably the most common defect in the western United States) or other leaks, pipe corrosion, or other similar faulty construction or materials.
- **Toxic molds.** This frequently is related to "sick building syndrome."
- **Mass-produced items.** Items mass-produced off-site such as windows, plumbing fixtures, siding, furnaces, and other building components also can be faulty.
- Also see our website at www.constructiondefects.com.

What Went Wrong, and Why?

Experts attempt to discover not only what is defective but also, and importantly, why it is defective. For example, a homeowner may notice a wall stain. The homeowner knows it is a sign of a defect, but does not know whether it is caused by a roof, deck, window or skylight, or other water leak; a sewage leak; growing mold, or simply the result of a bad paint job. Perhaps a problem seen on the outside of a building is being caused by something inside the building.

Diagnosing the cause of a problem requires considerable skill. Sometimes it is similar to determining the cause of an automobile engine malfunction. Six people can listen to an engine and come up with six different possible explanations for it, all of which are wrong. An expert mechanic can listen to the engine, run a few tests, and tell the owner what is wrong with the engine and how much it will cost to repair. The expert mechanic may initially cost more, but in the long run will be less expensive because of the mechanic's accuracy. As a mechanic friend of ours says, "I get paid $2 to tighten a bolt, but $50 to know which bolt to tighten and the best way to tighten it."

The expert may have to investigate the local building codes and national or regional industry standards as they existed at the time of construction. The developer may have met the codes and standards but still has built a defective building because the standards were too low. If the builder failed to meet government standards, it can be good evidence of a defect, although you need to have other information as evidence to prove your damages.

Exactly What are "Damages"?

Damages are any physical problems directly or indirectly related to the defects. These are termed "resultant damages" and include hidden damages. A good example is defective roofing. It is apparent that a leak discolored the walls and flooded the living room. However, the leak also may have resulted in rotting framing or mold and mildew that caused an allergic reaction in a member of the household.

Sometimes, to find all the resultant damages, parts of the house must be torn apart to perform "invasive" or "destructive" tests. Of course, these tests should be limited because of the inconvenience and costs involved. Testing about twenty percent of randomly selected homes in an affected tract or building generally will be enough.

How to Fix It

The experts or consultants next make repair suggestions and provide them to your attorney. These recommendations are usually very specific, and will include the repair plan or drawings, particular materials needed, scope of the work to be done, the types of workers or professionals needed, and any other information necessary to a contractor for making a cost estimate.

Receiving an accurate repair cost estimate is a vital part of the resolution of any construction defect claim. It is important not to underestimate the cost of repair, but equally important not to overestimate or "gold plate" the repair cost. Gold plating can cause your case to lose credibility with everyone involved and provide the opposition with an easily identifiable set of facts to undermine your case. It also can delay early settlement opportunities.

However, determining what constitutes "gold plating" varies with the techniques used for the original construction and the quality of the construction. For example, a homeowner with an asphalt roof that leaks because of poor installation probably cannot demand the roof be replaced with a more expensive concrete tile one. The homeowner does, however, have the right to a properly installed asphalt roof that does not leak. However, if the original materials themselves were faulty, the homeowner probably has the right to have the roof replaced with better materials, even if they are more expensive.

It is, therefore, imperative that your construction defect attorney be familiar with repair cost estimates. Even a small repair cost mistake can destroy your case or mean you will recover much less money than you need.

Chapter Three Do's and Don'ts

Do:

- Do always hire your experts and consultants through your attorney. Otherwise, you could lose confidentiality.

- Do give your attorney every bit of documentation that may be even remotely related to a defect.

- Do familiarize yourself with the numbers and types of experts that may be required.

- Do promptly fill out and respond to any forms or surveys your attorney or experts may send to you.

- Do familiarize yourself with your maintenance responsibilities and the responsibilities of your homeowner association. Read your CC&R's (Covenants Conditions and Restrictions).

Don't:

- Don't forget you may be responsible for your experts' fees and costs. Get a preliminary estimate before you start.

- Don't attempt to analyze the nature and cause of your problems yourself. This is why experts are hired.

- Don't "gold plate" your repairs.

Common Types of Construction Defects

Failing Flashing

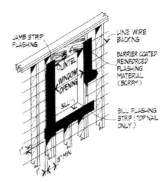

Flashing used to seal windows during installation will leak if the manufacturer's instructions are not followed. The damage can include water seeping into the home resulting in mold, mildew and fungal damage.

Mold and Where It Grows

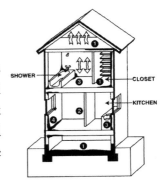

All mold needs to call your home its home is moisture, stagnant air to inhibit drying, and something—such as dust, soil or carpet fiber—to grow on. Allergies, asthma, and other health problems can than plague the building's occupants.

The Four Reasons Tile Roofs Leak

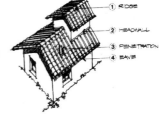

Look for improper installation at the ridge, headwall, internal vents, and eaves.

The Four Reasons Flat Roofs Leak

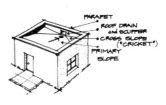

If water doesn't drain off and away from your home, it will drain inside your home. Watch for ponding water and leaks at the parapet, the roof drain, the cross slope, or the primary slope.

Moisture, Vapor and Slabs

A home with a weak foundation isn't much of a building at all. If a slab is not properly sealed, moisture can enter from just about anywhere—above, below, inside or outside.

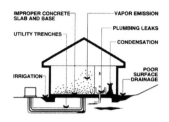

Framing Fungus and Other Rotting Stories

Whenever wood meets moisture where there is not proper ventilation to dry the wood out, fungus can, and most likely will, grow. Watch for (1) fungus at stair treads, (2) foundation posts and crawl spaces, (3) stair stringers, and (4) wood balcony railings.

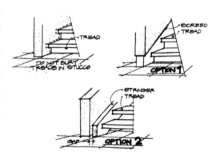

Visible Stucco Cracks

Stucco cracks primarily for two reasons. First, if the material is improperly installed, it will crack from expansion and contraction. Second, outside forces such as earthquakes, land-subsidence, and soil expansion can cause stucco cracks.

CHAPTER FOUR: WHAT THE CONSUMER SHOULD WATCH FOR

While it is the experts' jobs to find, define, locate, and estimate costs, there are items for which consumers should watch. It is nearly impossible to list all items, but we are providing a general list below. If you notice a potential defect, you should notify either your attorney or your homeowner association. While it is a complicated matter to decide whether or not a homeowner association should be notified, you should be able to determine what to do by examining the Covenants, Conditions, and Restrictions (CC&Rs), association rules and your deed. Look specifically for association and owner maintenance responsibilities sections.

Reading these documents can be a difficult process. They are written in very technical "legalese," which is nearly indecipherable to non-lawyers and even to lawyers who do not practice in the area. You should consult an attorney familiar with homeowner association law and construction defect law. Many different legal issues could be involved and a careful reading is required. Indeed, it is probably a good idea to have a qualified attorney review these documents before purchasing a home.

First Steps To Resolution

It may be the association's job, usually through the board of directors, to bring a claim. As a result, the safest answer is that if a homeowner association exists, or if the association is managed by a property management company, and the homeowner or resident suspects a defect, the homeowner should notify the association and property management company immediately in writing. There are numerous statutes of limitations and they frequently differ by state, which can limit how long you have for filing your complaint. If you miss the deadline, your lawsuit immediately fails.

Signs of Defects

Among the items to watch for are:

- Any sign of moisture or water leakage inside your home
- Dry rot anywhere
- Windows or doors that do not close correctly
- Ponding water or flooding outside your home
- Cracks in drywall, tile work, cabinets, and concrete slabs or foundations
- External stucco cracking, flaking or staining
- Odd smells and odors
- Lights that flicker on and off
- Loose, slipping, or falling roof tiles
- Power breaker switches that flip on and off on their own
- Absence of gutters and downspouts
- Water seeping through the slab
- Pest infestations through cracks in slabs or walls
- Uneven or sloping floors, or walls out of plumb
- Mold or mildew
- Stains on walls or ceilings
- Decks that don't drain properly, feel spongy, or have cracks on the surface
- Sidewalks, driveways or garage slabs that crack, have efflorescence, or begin to disintegrate
- Balcony railings that are loose, rusting, or rotting
- External patios and walls separating from house or slab
- Irrigation systems (usually sprinklers) that cause flooding or water ponding
- Wet slabs or moisture in crawl spaces

- Openings in attic crawl spaces between units
- Unusual sounds or considerable creaking at night
- Chimney caps without spark arrestors
- Dizziness, drowsiness, or an unusual number of colds or allergy symptoms you did not have before you moved into the building
- Extremely hot water that scalds on contact
- Gas ranges that fail to light, or burn sporadically, indicating leaky gas lines
- Heating systems and furnaces that fail to operate, or make unusual noises
- Lack of water pressure

Should You Tell the Developer?

Should you also notify the developer? Many owners and associations do, and if units are still being sold, the developer or the developer's representatives often sit on the board of directors until all housing is sold.

However, especially in new property, unless the defect is minor, such as an improperly tacked down carpet, or the developer sits on the board of directors, the general answer is not to tell the developer, because the developer will usually attempt the cheapest and quickest repair possible. This quick fix seldom is the best answer to the problem.

The Builder Warranty Myth

Many times, builders and developers represent that they are providing a complete warranty for the home. Most likely, this is not true. Seldom do these warranties provide complete protection, and they usually have very short expiration dates.

The important thing to remember is not to take the builder's word on what the warranty covers and doesn't cover, and to realize that your legal rights almost always far exceed what the builder's warranty provides. (See Appendix D.) Many homeowners, upon discovering a defect, will read their warranty and based upon that warranty decide that either the warranty has expired or does not cover whatever defect they suspect.

Don't fall into this trap. If you suspect a defect, consult your attorney to find out if redress exists. Don't consult the developer, who quite possibly will tell you that the warranty "does not cover" whatever defect it is, when, in fact, the law may allow for a wide array of compensation possibilities. As the proverbial "ounce of prevention," it might be a good idea for you to have your attorney read the warranty and all purchase documents before you close the deal on a new home.

Binding Arbitration Provisions in CC&R's

CC&R's frequently contain binding arbitration provisions. This means that if you have a dispute with the developer over a construction defect, you may be forced to have the matter heard and decided by an arbitrator rather than by a judge in court. (See page 75 for a discussion of arbitration.)

Before finalizing the purchase of your new home, again, it would be prudent to have your attorney explain to you the clauses contained in your CC&R's and what traps may lurk within them.

Maintenance and Repair Requirements

Again, you have a responsibility to maintain your property and keep it in good repair. Your CC&R's may spell out those requirements. For example, your CC&R's and other instructions you received with your new home may specify how patio surfaces must be maintained and what type of patio furniture is safe for the patio surface. Another example is that instructions with the home may advise that you water your lawn periodically but very deeply. One homeowner we know watered his lawn too frequently and too shallowly. The result was that the trees in his front yard sent out shallow roots and he was forced to replace his entire front lawn at his own cost.

Monthly Assessments

In some developments, whether the homes are freestanding single homes or condos, you may be billed monthly by the homeowner association.

These fees are not optional. If you fail to pay them, your property title could be attached by the homeowner association, and potentially, your home could be sold to recoup the assessment arrearages. The funds are used by homeowner associations to keep common areas in good repair and to pay other common costs such as lawyer fees. Indeed, the assessment may be increased to make emergency repairs before or during litigation, or to otherwise specially fund litigation.

Every state requires you to "mitigate" your damages, or, in other words, you have to do what's reasonable to prevent your damages from getting worse and to repair them, if possible, before or during the course of a claim.

Low-ball it

Frequently, homeowners inform a developer of a problem and the developer claims he will repair it or pay to have it repaired. He then proceeds to "low-ball" the repair, which means either perform the cheapest work possible or pay to have the cheapest work possible performed. He may do so under the guise of his written express warranty. (See Appendix D.) Remember, you have the right to the home you thought you were buying and the one you were either implicitly or explicitly promised.

Chapter Four Do's and Don'ts

Do:

- Do have your attorney examine your Covenants, Conditions and Restrictions if there is a question of whether your homeowner association should be notified.

- Do be familiar with potential defects. Among the categories are: leaking windows, doors and roofs, exterior stucco and siding defects, improper drainage, design defects, poor materials selection, faculty construction techniques, mold and mildew, and faulty mass-produced items.

Don't:

- Don't tell the developer of a defect unless your attorney directs you to do so.

- Don't let the developer make repairs unless you know the fix is permanent.

- Don't try to handle warranty claims yourself; the builder is better trained and financed.

- Don't let the developer make "Band-Aid" repairs. The defects will reappear next year.

CHAPTER FIVE: THE RIGHT LAWYER AND EXPERTS

Proving the existence of a latent or patent defect is an arduous task requiring expert investigation and analysis. Effective coordination among homeowners, property managers, consultants, experts, and legal counsel is crucial to a successful defect case. The lawyer usually assumes the responsibility of creating and maintaining these relationships. In addition, construction defect lawsuits are among the most complex in the legal field. As a result, retaining the best possible legal counsel can make or break a case.

Finding the Right Lawyer

Frequently, both homeowner associations and individual homeowners are involved in hiring lawyers. When homeowner associations are making the decision, the property management company and the association's corporate counsel usually suggest or recommend legal counsel. When individual homeowners are the only potential plaintiffs, it becomes their personal responsibility to hire counsel. In either case, the principles and methods employed are basically the same.

You should meet with several different firms and obtain proposals from them. Review and evaluate each law firm's qualifications. Rate each on the basis of their knowledge of construction defect law (especially when homeowner associations are involved), trial and mediation experience, track record, settlement history, reputation, integrity, and fees.

Obtain and check references. Let the attorneys know who most likely will be bringing the action and who will be sued, so the lawyers can make sure they have no conflicts of interest. Legal counsel has an ethical responsibility to disclose any potential conflict of interest in writing. For example, a law firm that once represented the developer would not be a wise choice even if the firm disclosed this and requested a waiver from the homeowner or homeowner association. Also, a firm that has no conflict of interest but has represented developers in the past should be carefully scrutinized.

Construction defect claims usually require many hours of work by numerous attorneys, paralegals, and other support staff. Because of this, it is important to ensure that the firm you select is large enough and staffed well enough to handle the work. A firm that is financially strong has more staying power and can more easily finance the legal and expert costs. Interview the lawyer who will be running the case, and also the firm's senior attorney, especially for large, complex cases where homeowner associations are involved.

Avoid hiring an attorney who is a homeowner, member of the homeowner association, or who has a close personal relationship with a board member. The association's general counsel should not be hired. You need him to remain impartial and provide needed checks and balances. Instead, corporate counsel should be involved in hiring the defect lawyer. Never use the corporate counsel in the pre-litigation process because this could result in a conflict of interest in certain cases. Also, avoid an attorney who works both sides of the fence or works for insurance companies. There is no way of knowing how an attorney's judgement will be affected by these dual allegiances. See Appendix B for a checklist on hiring an attorney.

Attorney-Client Privilege

Any communications between attorneys and clients are privileged when they involve the underlying action or potential lawsuit. It is vital, therefore, that you, as a client, understand the sensitive nature of the information and not discuss the case with anyone except your attorney or his agent. You and your attorney should set up a procedure for communicating without divulging the information to a third party. One effective method is to have counsel communicate with a designated board officer or litigation committee before each board meeting. The contact then can report to the board in an executive session. Of course, if you are a sole homeowner bringing suit, you should deal directly with the law firm.

When multiple homeowners are plaintiffs in one action, each homeowner should maintain a separate file. Address invoices from retained consultants to your attorney, and forward them to the management company, which also should maintain a file separate from the rest of the association's files and documents.

What the Attorney Does

In construction defect cases, the attorney is responsible for more than just recovering damages. His job also is to advise whether or not you have a case in the first place. Competent and ethical attorneys will not take cases in which there is little to no chance of recovery. Contrary to popular myth, ethical attorneys do not want to put the time, effort and money into a pointless lawsuit just to bill you for fees. Trial lawyers like to actually win their cases.

The attorney also must make recommendations on commencing the claim process, retaining consultants, alternative repair methods, available contractors, and the applicable statutes of limitations. Frequently, the attorney is asked to help obtain financing for repairs and may also be requested to assess a settlement proposal that calls for responsible parties to perform needed repairs.

The attorney's role as advisor calls for understanding construction problems, solutions beyond court actions, and the after-trial process. In a construction defect case, the lawyer may represent hundreds of clients and is responsible to each. Most associations have general counsel to respond to questions association members may have regarding board member responsibilities, financing, standing to sue, interpreting governing documents, allocating association reserves, contracting consultants, settlement sufficiency, and reconstruction.

Tasks your law firm should perform include:

- Initial due diligence and fiduciary duty case review. This is the first task your attorney will undertake. It includes:

- An onsite preliminary inspection by consultants and experts to determine the existence of any defects.
- A meeting with the Board of Directors and management company (or individual homeowners, when applicable) to discuss legal options.
- A survey of all homeowners to determine the extent and scope of the defects, and a full report.
- A thorough review of all documents and files to prepare a statute of limitations analysis.
- Conducting site visits with select independent experts to verify existing common-area problems and consumer complaints.
- Developing a preliminary budget regarding expert investigations.
- Meeting again with the board of directors to discuss findings and recommendations.
- Attending monthly board meetings as required or requested.
- Sending monthly status letters.
- Sending a monthly budget report and updates.

- Update individual homeowner or association board of directors on new state regulations and case law.
- Assist in locating reconstruction experts and provide findings and recommendations after a settlement or verdict.
- Estimate all financial expenditures.
- Attend annual homeowner association meetings and update members.
- Help find financing for necessary repairs that must be undertaken before settlement or judgment.

What's It Going to Cost?

In some states, such as California, attorney fees usually cannot be recovered from the defendants, while in other states, such as Nevada and Arizona, fees can be recovered at trial. In either case, carefully consider and review the potential fees and costs. Except in a few special cases, fees are seldom set by law; they are negotiated between the lawyer and client. Do not hesitate to negotiate. In the case of homeowner associations, the association makes the final decision on the attorney-client relationship, and the association's general or corporate counsel should review the proposed fee agreement. Do not hire the assocation's general counsel law firm to handle your construction defect claim. It often poses a conflict of interest.

In most states, contingency fee agreements must comply with statutes and court rules. These laws and rules typically require that all agreements be in writing, that the client be provided with a copy of the agreement, and that the client be notified that the fees are negotiable. If the attorney fails to meet the mandatory requirements, the client can rescind the agreement.

There are various ways fees can be set up. Among them are:

- **Pure contingency.** This means the attorney receives a percentage of any recovery (most common). Under this arrangement, the attorney takes on all the risk. If there is no recovery, you owe no fees. Most homeowners and associations do not have the funds to battle the developer and are not willing to be responsible for paying lawyers' bills monthly for two or more years.

- **Pure hourly.** This means the fee is a set hourly rate. Usually, different attorneys in a law firm bill at different rates depending on whether the lawyer is a partner or associate and how much experience the particular attorney has. In addition, firms usually bill for paralegal time (least common).

- **Hybrid hourly and contingency.** This can be complex, but generally a lawyer will reduce his hourly rate in exchange for a lower contingency fee. For example, an attorney may cut his hourly rate in half in exchange for also receiving half his normal contingency fee (seldom used).

Problems occur when the responsible party agrees to repair the property instead of making a cash payment. Occasionally, defendants agree to buy back the property. In those situations, who pays the attorney and experts?

If this is the situation, your attorney should negotiate fees and expert costs separately so the homeowner association is made whole. If that fails, the homeowner association should prioritize repairs and fix the major problems causing ongoing property damage (water or soil settlement cracks) and present life or safety issues. Fee agreements should include language stating that reasonable attorney fees can be recovered and will be paid to your lawyer. In a buy-back situation, the agreement should base the fees on the reasonable value of the property that is repurchased. The agreement should also include a provision for arbitration should a fee agreement not be reached.

Changing Attorneys

The client almost always has the absolute legal right to fire his attorney and hire another. When the client does fire the attorney, however, the lawyer still has a right to "reasonable fees" for his work because it is hardly fair to have one lawyer to spend what could be years to work up a case, only to have another step in and take the fees. These fees for the first lawyer will come out of any settlement or judgment eventually achieved, or he will be due his hourly rate up to the time of discharge. Generally, hourly rates must be paid at the time of discharge. In contingency fee cases, the attorney waits for a portion of the settlement or judgment. It is important for you to tell your replacement counsel of the previous attorney and any fees that must come out of the new lawyer's contingency fee. You also can negotiate with your new lawyer to pay directly the costs and fees of your previous lawyer.

It is never too late to make changes and don't ever think you are in too deep. Getting another attorney's opinion is free and should give you greater insight into your case at the very least. Lawyers often have very different ways of viewing a case.

Chapter Five Do's and Don'ts

Do:

• Do meet with several law firms and obtain separate proposals from each.

• Do evaluate and review a law firm's basic knowledge and experience with construction defect cases, trial and mediation experience, track record, settlement history, reputation, integrity, fees, and advancing expert costs.

- Do tell your attorney of all potential plaintiffs and defendants so he or she can check for conflicts of interest.

- Do check references.

- Do check to see if the potential law firm is large enough and has the staff resources and finances to effectively pursue the claim.

- Do establish a protocol to efficiently and effectively communicate with your attorney to maintain confidentiality.

- Do maintain a separate file for each homeowner if multiple home-owners are pursuing claims.

- Do carefully negotiate fees.

- Do make sure the fee agreement makes allowances for alternate set-tlement methods such as buy-backs and developer-conducted repairs.

Don't:

- Don't hesitate to have a second attorney give an opinion, even if your attorney has already made a claim or filed suit.

- Don't hire an attorney who is a homeowner in your development or is an association member.

- Don't hire the association's corporate or general counsel law firm to pursue a construction defect claim.

- Don't hire an attorney just because he or she has a close personal rela-tionship with a board member.

- Don't limit yourself by your first choice of attorneys; if you are not satisfied, change.

- Don't hire an attorney who also works for builders, contractors or insurance companies.

CHAPTER SIX:
FINANCING THE LAWSUIT

Depending on the number of plaintiffs or the size of the homeowner association, financing a lawsuit can cost big bucks. Experts and other fees and costs can be very high. Homeowner associations and homeowners may have to make temporary repairs, and homeowners may be forced to relocate because of health hazards or because the housing is not habitable.

Raising the Money

Raising the necessary money to pay costs and fees can place the homeowner in a tough financial situation. However, there are ways to pay for it all without going broke in the process. Among them are:

- **Litigation counsel**. Most experienced construction defect attorneys will finance costs on cases they handle. This may be the only way single-family homeowners can pay these costs. It is important to remember that these fees must be repaid to the attorney even if there is no settlement or other recovery.

- **Liens**. Some experts will perform their work and agree to place a lien on any recovery. However, again it is important to remember that even if there is no recovery, the money is still owed.

- **Association reserves**. The law in many states allows the use of common interest association reserve funds to pursue claims related to property repair, restoration, replacement, or maintenance. Reserve funds also may be transferred to general operating accounts to meet short-term cash flow problems. Of course, the transferred funds must be returned to the reserve fund, usually within a set time period unless the association extends the time limits. The association may create a special assessment to return the funds.

- **Loans**. Since few associations have collateral for loans, it is often a challenge to borrow money. However, many lending institutions will make loans to associations with good credit records. Veteran association lawyers are familiar with lenders and usually know who will make these loans. An individual homeowner can generally go to their original lender, who will be interested in maintaining the value of the home because it is the collateral for the original loan.

- **Special assessments**. Many association CC&Rs require a vote to pass a special assessment because raising dues is limited, usually to five percent. Passing a special assessment can be an alternative method of financing litigation costs.

Is the Developer Able to Pay?

Before proceeding, a competent lawyer will make sure the developer or other potential defendant has the resources to pay a settlement or judgment. Even if the developer or other defendants are no longer in business, there may be insurance available to satisfy a judgment. However, it makes little sense to expend the time, effort, and expense of suit if it is impossible to collect.

Also, your attorney should explain his litigation plan. He or she will investigate every member of the developer's team and will need access to any information you may have in your files, such as brochures, warranties, sales information, or governmental filings. Providing this information will aid your lawyer in pursuing your claim. This information also will help your lawyer discover potential defendants. Developers often form corporations to build homes, and then, when the homes are completed, they collapse the corporation. After that, tracking who is responsible for what is a more difficult task.

A skilled attorney also may be able to entirely circumvent the need for litigation. Insurance companies and developers usually know the heavyweight construction defect lawyers. After evaluating the case and your legal counsel, they may decide to cut their losses and settle the case. This is especially true when the experts and consultants have conducted an effective investigation and your attorney can present a persuasive argument. Not only should you question your attorney about previous trial results, but also about settlements, because only about five percent of cases ever go to trial.

Chapter Six Do's and Don'ts

Do:

- Do have your attorney ascertain if the developer has assets or insurance to pay a claim.

- Do have your attorney explain the various methods of financing a lawsuit.

Don't:

- Don't proceed without carefully analyzing all litigation costs.

CHAPTER SEVEN: WHO CAN SUE?

Homeowners

Historically, only the property owner who bought the property directly from the developer had the right to legal redress. The original buyer was said to have "privity," a direct contract relationship, with the developer. Therefore, with the right to the property's possession, the original purchaser was said to be the "real party in interest." Recent legal changes, however, have allowed both homeowner associations and subsequent buyers to bring suit.

However, problems often arise in determining who gets to recover if the property changes hands during litigation. Is it the person who owned the property at the beginning of the action, or is it the person who owned the property when the case was completed?

In California, the general rule is the person whose interest is injured from the defect is the person who has the right to the lawsuit recovery. This can become very complex, and depends on the facts of each situation. For example, someone who owned the property at the beginning of the suit and sold the property during the middle of litigation, but received less than full value of the property because of the claim, has the right to compensation. Conversely, someone who sold the property for full value has no such rights.

The moral of the story is this: If you sell the property during the action, in most states you must disclose that the property is involved in litigation and you should, through your broker, real estate agent, or lawyer, discuss and agree with the buyer which party has the right to recover. The results of this discussion should be put into writing and included your sales contract.

Can Homeowner Associations Bring Suit?

In the last few decades, the number of common interest developments and condominiums has increased dramatically. The question arises if homeowner associations, as a single entity, can bring action for faulty construction. As in most issues involving the law and lawyers, it depends.

Common interest developments include condominiums, stock cooperatives, and projects with homeowner associations, and are usually defined as "non-profit mutual benefit associations created for the purpose of managing a common interest development." They do have the right to bring suit, but what they can sue for usually depends on how the property is owned.

For example, houses built on separate lots are usually owned by private buyers, not the homeowner association, while common areas within the development, such as swimming pools, clubhouses, and play areas, may be owned or leased by the homeowner association. Who can sue for what depends on who owns what, and the CC&Rs will help you define responsibilities. Each owner is probably responsible for his or her own property, but the association most likely will have to make the claim for common area defects.

In apartment-style condominium projects the answer becomes even more complex. Usually, in condominiums the walls and other structures are owned by the homeowner association or cooperative, while the homeowners own only their "air-space," internal walls, carpeting, and fixtures. Therefore, the homeowner association is usually the entity that brings construction defect lawsuits.

Some developments, such as duplexes and triplexes, have a hybrid system. The general principles still apply, however, and you can sue only for what you own. For example, in duplexes, individual owners may own certain walls, but not front yards or back yards adjacent to their property.

In most states, if the potential exists for a lawsuit to be brought by the homeowner association, the board of directors has a duty to investigate the situation and, if a defect exits, bring the lawsuit. If the board of directors fails to do so, the board can be held liable, and in some instances, the individual directors can be held liable. This is why it is important that the association have "errors and omissions" insurance coverage.

Before deciding who can be plaintiffs, your lawyer must carefully examine all pertinent documents and recordings.

Class Action

Class action lawsuits allow large numbers of "similarly situated" homeowners to bring a claim as one unit. For example, if all or most homes in a single-family home development are built with substandard roofing that results in leaks, all of the affected homeowners can sue as a class.

Usually, one homeowner, who should be one of the original owners, is the named plaintiff who is the "class representative." The procedure becomes fairly complex. First, the "class" must be court-certified as proper. Certifying the class is not as simple as it may sound. Courts vary radically on what they will certify, and developers will fight certification because they want to limit the number of potential claimants. However, class action is the preferred method of proceeding in a single-family housing development since it allows all the owners to bring a claim at the same time. Often, if individual claims are brought, many owners do not get involved because of apathy, embarrassment, the need to sell or refinance, or other reasons, even though they share a common construction defect with other homeowners. Members of the class, along with the representative, must be shown to share well-defined issues of law and fact.

In addition, attorneys usually must meet certain qualifications before courts will allow them to be lead counsel representing plaintiffs in class action lawsuits. Individual class members who desire to bring their claims separately from the class must "opt out" of the class.

Of course, homeowners in an apartment-style condominium do not need to file a class-action because the principal building owner is the homeowner association and it brings the lawsuit.

Attorney fees and costs frequently are handled differently in class action lawsuits than in individual lawsuits. In some jurisdictions, the losing party can be required to pay the prevailing party's attorney fees and other costs. In some jurisdictions, the plaintiffs will be liable individually for the defendant's fees and costs if the plaintiffs fail to prevail. Prudent clients will require that their attorneys carefully and completely explain these possibilities.

Chapter Seven Do's and Don'ts

Do:

- Do have your attorney decide if the homeowner association, individual homeowners, or both should bring suit.

- Do understand that the term "Homeowner Association" can include many different ownership entities such as Common Interest Development, Condominiums, Townhomes, and Homeowner Associations that own common areas.

- Do have your attorney explain what the individual homeowners own and what the homeowner association owns.

Don't:

- Don't fail to carefully explain to potential buyers if you are in the middle of a defect dispute and who will receive any recovery. Put such information in the purchase agreement.

CHAPTER EIGHT: STEPS BEFORE THE DANCE BEGINS

A competent attorney's goal usually is to settle the case before litigation begins. Early settlement can save claimants considerable sums of money and can reduce defense costs. As a result, many states across the nation have instituted statutory schemes to encourage pre-litigation resolution.

These schemes are almost always extremely complex and are full of pitfalls for the unwary. Your attorney must carefully guide you, step by step. This is yet another reason you should be sure your attorney is experienced in construction defect litigation and has the resources to punctiliously research the issues involved.

In addition, each of these schemes contains rigid time frames. Meeting the deadlines requires a law firm that is capable of acting quickly and with considerable skill. These time frames are another reason you should notify your attorney and your homeowner association as soon as you notice a potential defect.

Most of these schemes were created at the request of the insurance and development industry, tend to favor these industries, and are strongly opposed by most consumer groups. However, they also can aid homeowners by providing the framework for negotiations. Pre-litigation statutory schemes vary from state to state, but have some similarities. Examining a few of them should provide an idea of how they operate. For example, California, Arizona, Nevada, and Oregon recently have imposed new measures that must be taken before filing construction defect lawsuits.

The California Way

The California statute requires homeowners to notify the developer of specific defects. The developer then has the right to inspect the property and make offers to repair or settle. The homeowners may accept or reject the offers. Only after rejecting the offers may the homeowners bring suit.

The process is rife with complications and full of potential landmines for the unwary. There are deadlines that must be met, and special meetings must be held within set time limits. Prudence requires that you use competent, experienced legal counsel. In addition, you may be exempt from these requirements. Careful legal analysis is required to determine whether or not you must comply.

The Nevada System

Nevada's legal requirements are similar to California's. However, Nevada requires certain steps be taken concurrent with litigation, and mandatory mediation also is required here. Again, it is a labyrinth of deadlines, conferences, timelines, inspections, paperwork and more paperwork, and requires careful and experienced legal analysis.

Life in Arizona

Arizonans have taken another path. Their law requires homeowner associations, but not homeowners, to take particular steps before beginning a lawsuit. Arizona law also places special responsibility on homeowner association boards of directors to keep association members informed. They must disclose information about the litigation, such as the nature of the action, how it will be filed, how it will be financed, what demands will be made on the builder, how the builder responded, and numerous other items. In addition, the association's board of directors cannot authorize bringing legal action until after the homeowners meet with the board of directors.

The Oregon Trail

Oregon's law covers class action lawsuits. It requires that thirty days before filing suit, the class representative must notify all the defendants by registered return-request mail as to what the causes of action are, and demand that the defendants correct or rectify the alleged wrong. It is important to remember that the Oregon pre-litigation statute does not toll the statute of limitations (stop the time clock from ticking), which means you must act promptly.

The Lone Star State

In Texas, as usual, they do things their own way. Texas law says that a claimant must mail the contractor a written list of the suspected defects. You must send this notice, following specific mailing procedures, more than sixty days before filing a construction defect lawsuit. The contractor then has 45 days after receiving the notice to make a written settlement offer.

The law in this area is constantly changing and evolving. Generally, insurance companies and building groups want to make the process more difficult, with fewer consumer remedies for faulty construction. Conversely, consumer groups such as Consumer Attorneys of California and Homeowners Against Deficient Dwellings attempt to protect homeowners from faulty construction and give the consumer a greater number of remedies.

Remember, most of these pre-litigation statutory schemes were the result of extensive and expensive governmental lobbying by the insurance and real estate industries that have a seemingly endless supply of time and money at their disposal. The requirements are therefore slanted against the consumer in an attempt to make pursuing a claim as difficult as possible. This is yet another reason to rely on competent legal counsel.

Chapter Eight Do's and Don'ts

Do:

- Do promptly provide any information your lawyer needs to complete any statutorily required pre-litigation steps.

- Do familiarize yourself with whatever pre-litigation steps your jurisdiction may have.

- Do act promptly. Many states have complex time limits on pre-litigation steps.

Don't:

- Don't procrastinate in doing what your attorney has asked.

- Don't act slowly. You must meet the deadlines, or you could lose your right to your claim.

- Don't believe the builder has your interests in mind.

CHAPTER NINE: WHAT LAWYERS ARGUE TO COLLECT

Construction defect legal theories have taken centuries to develop, are influenced by—and sometimes created by—a myriad set of state statutes, and can be, even for the most skilled attorney, difficult to understand. We have written several legal textbooks that have attempted to explain these issues to lawyers, and even then the competent lawyer will need nearly an entire library to skillfully prosecute a construction defect case. In addition, the law is a growing and evolving organism and nearly always in a state of flux.

However, the consumer involved in a construction defect claim should have a basic understanding of the legal theories and principles involved so that when a lawyer says something, one understands what is being said. While there are too many theories to be listed and outlined here, the most common ones are:

Strict Liability

Under strict liability, one need not prove anyone was at fault. As discussed previously the argument for the institution for strict liability is that consumers seldom can be expected to know as much about mass marketed and massed produced, technologically sophisticated housing as the producer and manufacturer.

For example, when a home buyer flips a light switch he or she cannot be expected to understand the relationship of current to voltage (the two are inversely proportional and total power equals voltage times amperage, or $P = I \times E$), or which wiring types work the best and last the longest (gold and platinum, but copper is the best substitute), or what wiring diameter is required to carry a certain load (depends on voltage, current and type of wiring), or the size of an electron, or whether parallel or series circuitry works the best in homes (generally parallel), or the atomic theory behind nuclear power and quark theory (beats us, but it has something to do with spin and *Finnegan's Wake*). One shouldn't even be required to know the difference between direct current, DC, or alternating current, AC. DC goes directly from negative to positive, while AC shifts polarity in a sine wave according to its frequency. Household current is AC, 120 volts, and shifts 60 times every second.

What one needs to know is that when one flips the switch, the lamp is supposed to produce light. If it doesn't, and the light bulb isn't burnt out, and the lamp is plugged in, there could be a defect.

Besides not having to show fault, another advantage of strict liability is that one need not be the original buyer who made the contract with the developer; this is called "being in privity" with the developer. One can be the tenth buyer and still bring suit under strict liability so long as it is done within a statutory time.

The ability of a later purchaser to make a construction defect claim is very important. We live in an increasingly mobile society and it is not unusual for people to move household every few years, especially in an appreciating home market.

Frequently, however, defects do not manifest themselves for a number of years. For example, a home in a climate with little rain will not suffer roof leaks until there is a moderately wet season. It could take several years for a latent roof defect to become apparent. Another example is a beam or joist that is cracked when installed. It may take several years for the beam or joist to fail.

Strict liability requires only that the house, condominium, or manufactured component such as window or furnace, is defective and that the defect causes damage. The defect can be in design, site selection, engineering, workmanship, materials, construction technique, or a plethora or other things. The most frequent cause of a defect is a home not built in accord with the approved plans and specifications, industry design standards, or building code requirements. But under strict liability there is no need to identify which designer, engineer, or contractor was in error. One need simply prove a defect in a mass produced house.

Breach of Implied Warranty

The implied warranty of merchantability was the first intrusion into the old doctrine of *caveat emptor*. "Implied" means the warranty is not written nor otherwise expressed. Basically, it means when one buys a home, it is implied the house should be habitable. For example, a buyer reasonably expects the lights to work, the roof to keep water out, and the house not to fall down a hill.

The "breach of implied warranty" legal theory is used in those states that have not attached strict liability, when the statute of limitations has expired, or when the house was not a mass-produced consumer item. Many states, such as California, Nevada, and Arizona, have extended implied warranty to later purchasers, subject to the various states' statutes of limitations.

Breach of Express Warranty

Many developers include written, express warranties within sales contracts. This is similar to a warranty one receives on an automobile. Also, as with a car, an express warranty is enforceable only by the original purchaser unless the warranty states otherwise.

Note that, simply because a purchasing agreement states you have a two-year warranty or guarantee does not mean you are limited to that number of years. Some homebuyers will discover a defect, then read the purchase agreement that says they only have a one or two-year warranty. They will assume the warranty has expired and not pursue the claim. This could be disastrous. Again, notify an attorney and your homeowner association (if appropriate) if you suspect a construction defect.

Negligence

As discussed on page three, negligence requires one to show the developer had a duty to build in a reasonable manner and breached that duty, causing damages. For example, a developer has a duty to use undamaged lumber. If the developer uses a cracked beam, and as a result the house collapses, the developer is probably negligent.

Negligence is often unnecessary against developers in states that have adopted strict liability causes of action. However, because many service professionals such as architects and engineers, brokers, property managers, and agents cannot be sued in strict liability (because they do not mass-produce a product), negligence still is an effective cause of action.

In addition, if a developer or builder negligently hired or supervised a subcontractor, the developer can be found liable in negligence.

Also, if the developer was the seller and broker, the developer can be held liable in negligence for failing to disclose building problems such as the expected creation of a nearby freeway. Plus, if the developer sits as a member of the homeowner association's board of directors—which in early development phases he usually does—and fails to perform a duty as a board member, such as filing a claim for construction defects against himself, he may be liable for negligence under the association's CC&Rs.

Fraud, Deceit, and Misrepresentation

Lawyers and legal scholars can spend lifetimes and millions of words distinguishing actual fraud from constructive fraud, and constructive fraud from intentional misrepresentation or deceit. Each has a highly technical meaning that means little to anyone except lawyers. Also, various statutes in various states provide various definitions for the same terms.

To save you the time, money, and effort of attending law school, studying for the Bar Exam, and hopefully passing it, we will provide very general and truncated definitions.

As a very general rule, each of the three is an omission of a known fact, or the statement as fact of something not true, that is relied upon and causes damages. For example, you purchase a home built atop a toxic dump and the seller knows the dump exists but either lies to you or fails to tell you about the dump. You rely upon these statements or omissions, and after you buy the home you grow a second right hand or cannot resell the property. You have been a victim of at least one of the items in this category.

The important thing is that you tell your lawyer everything you can think of about your injury so he or she can decide if a fraud, deceit, or misrepresentation has occurred.

Nuisance

Nuisance, the pain-in-the-neck cause of action, occurs when something is injurious to health, indecent, offensive to the senses, an obstruction to the enjoyment of life or property, or obstructs the free passage or use of a public right of way such as a lake, river, creek, street, or park.

The advantage of a nuisance theory is that it is a continuing tort, which means that as long as the nuisance exists, the time period for filing a complaint never runs out. For example, if on your twenty-fifth birthday you buy a new house that has an offensive odor, and that odor continues to smell, that possibly would be considered a continuing tort. If the odor continues for fifty years, you still might be able to bring a lawsuit on your seventh fifth birthday.

Of course, this is an extreme example, and it is doubtful courts would allow it, but courts do not like disallowing a valid claim just because one was a little late filing a complaint, and lawyers are always searching for ways to encourage judges to give people their day in court.

Multiple Causes of Action

Almost always, an attorney will allege more than one cause of action in a complaint. For example, he or she may claim the developer and others are liable in fraud, negligence, strict liability, nuisance, and violation of an implied warranty, then ask for compensatory and punitive damages (if permitted in the jurisdiction).

He or she will allege more than one cause of action for several reasons. First, some defendants may be liable for different things in different causes of actions. Second, there may be a statute of limitations problem that the attorney is deftly attempting to circumvent. Or, just because a developer is liable under strict liability, doesn't mean it isn't a good idea to show the judge and jury how the developer was negligent and what he or she did wrong. This could give your case more force. In addition, in a few causes of action, attorney fees are available where otherwise they might not be available.

Chapter Nine Do's and Don'ts

Do:

- Do learn some of the important terminology that applies to your case.

Don't:

- Don't be embarrassed to ask your lawyer questions if you don't understand something about your case.

CHAPTER TEN: INSURANCE

No consumer, just before signing the multi-page sales contract for his or her new home, is going to stop and ask the broker or agent if the developer has construction defect insurance. Nor do we suggest the buyer do so.

In most states, whether or not the developer and other defendants have insurance to cover the defects is usually an issue of utmost importance. Determining these issues should be left to your attorney.

However, consumers caught in the middle of a litigation should have a basic understanding of insurance and what the assorted insurance terms mean. Understanding the ins and outs of an insurance policy can make the difference between a great lawyer and a merely good one. Determining what insurance coverage is available and correctly tapping into its coverage often determines overall strategy within a lawsuit.

One of the most essential tasks of your attorney and the defense attorney is evaluating available insurance. Often, a developer either has no assets, or assets that are insufficient to cover damages, or the corporation the developer founded to fund the litigation has been dissolved. The presence of insurance coverage for the developer, builder, and subcontractors may be the only source of recovery for homeowners.

Because insurance companies and developers know defect cases can be expensive and may result in considerable losses, they frequently retain specialist attorneys to provide expert analysis of policies and insurance law in an attempt to avoid coverage.

Third-Party Claims

Third-party claims are the nucleus of most construction defect cases. When a homeowner sues a developer, the developer will pass the lawsuit to his insurance company. This makes the homeowner the third-party claimant. This, of course, assumes the developer, contractor, sub-contractor, or builder has insurance.

Coverage: The Big Question

The big question, and often a multi-million dollar one, is whether insurance is available. Insurance companies are in business to collect premiums, and not to pay claims. As a result, insurance companies will assert that damages do not exist, that they are not the client's fault and therefore not the client's responsibility, or that the particular insurance policy does not cover the damages in question.

States can vary on whether a developer's insurance will cover defects and exactly what constitutes coverable property damages. Courts in Arizona, California, Nevada, Oregon, Alaska, Texas, and Georgia have ruled that insurance will cover construction defects such as leaky roofs and cracked foundations. Courts in North Carolina and Hawaii appear to be undecided, and in other states, such as Illinois, Iowa and Florida the courts generally deny coverage.

Developers usually receive coverage from two sources. First, their own policies, and second, from the policies of the sub-contractors they hire. When those two policy sources are emptied, they usually have excess or umbrella coverage to provide money above the first two policies.

Successfully pursuing third-party claims requires your attorney to analyze numerous factors. First, he or she must understand the standard comprehensive policy and what it usually includes, and its endorsements. Secondly, he or she must understand the responsibilities among successive holders, excess, and umbrella insurance policies (a developer may have up to $1 million with one carrier and $1–2 million with another). Tertiary (we always wanted to use that word), your attorney must know what constitutes an "occurrence" (most policies say they will cover only so much money "per occurrence"), and lastly, what is and is not covered by the policy.

Most construction defect law firms have one or two attorneys who have either represented insurance companies or understand insurance coverage issues. Many of those attorneys have extensive insurance industry experience and know how insurance companies operate.

Reservation of Rights

When a claim is made against an insurance company, the company usually will make what is called a "reservation of rights." This means the insurer will investigate the claim, defend the insured in a lawsuit, but reserves the right to reject the claim or refuse to pay a judgment or verdict.

Insurance companies do this because the policy may exclude coverage, or what is claimed may not have occurred while the policy was in effect. Indeed, it may not be apparent until after the case is investigated and defended, and it also is possible that part of the alleged damages is covered and part is not.

Reservations of rights problems can be complex. Frequently, that the insurer reserved rights can itself result in litigation. Your carrier may decide it had no responsibility to defend your case and demand its costs and legal fees back.

Except in cross complaints (you sue the developer and the developer sues you back) and in rare other cases, seldom does one bringing a construction defect case receive a reservation of rights letter or enter into a reservation of rights contract. However, reservation of rights issues can influence how a case is brought. For example, few policies cover intentional fraud, other intentional acts, or punitive damages awards. Therefore, the wise attorney must be careful how he or she drafts the original complaint so that after legal action the insurance carrier will not announce that it will not cover the claim because the plaintiff showed that the defendant intentionally caused the damages and, therefore, the damages are not covered. Just because a jury awards $1 billion in punitive damages does not mean you will ever get a dime. It is far better to be awarded a smaller amount in recoverable damages.

Declaratory Relief

A declaratory relief action is brought when either the insured or insurer wants a court determination of whether the insurance company has a responsibility to defend an insured against a lawsuit or pay the defendant's damages, or both, before the case is settled or tried. A court also may rule on other related issues such as whether the insurance company must hire for the insured an independent lawyer with no connections to the insurance company.

Insurance Company Duties

An insurance company must reasonably investigate the claim and decide if it has a responsibility to defend the case or pay damages ("indemnify") for its insured before denying coverage. Since there is an obvious conflict between the insured's interests and the insurance company's interests, the insurance company has an "implied covenant of good faith and fair dealing" and is subject to a "bad faith" lawsuit, which includes punitive damages, if the insurance company fails to meet the requirements of good faith and fair dealing.

Insurance bad faith matters become very complicated in themselves. Who can sue for what varies from state to state and virtually from day to day. Competent legal counsel must carefully evaluate these cases. Insurance bad faith comes into play when the developer is still in business and his insurance company will not pony up the damage money. Sometimes you can settle with the developer and as part of the settlement he will assign any bad faith claim he may have against his insurance company.

Duty of Insured

Generally, the insured have certain duties. First is to give notice of the claim to the insurer within a certain time. Second, the insured must cooperate in the defense of a claim. Third, the insured cannot enter into a settlement agreement without the participation of his or her insurance company and then attempt to collect what the insured pays in the settlement from the insurance company.

Homeowner Insurance

Rarely will the homeowner association's policies cover damages unless you have disaster (earthquake, flood, hurricane) coverage. For example, suppose a developer built on or near an earthquake fault and failed to reinforce the house to survive an expected earthquake. If you are a homeowner with a Veterans Administration VA loan, you would be required by the VA to purchase earthquake insurance. Two months after the house is completed and you have moved in, the unexpected occurs and an earthquake destroys the house. Who pays?

The answer depends on a number of factors including, among other things, the damages, what your policy says, what the developer's policy says, what the homeowner association's policy says, and what each policy covers. Standard homeowner policies will not cover emotional distress or faulty design, workmanship or materials that caused damage. Your policy may not cover full repair costs, or may prohibit rebuilding on that particular location.

Chapter Ten Do's and Don'ts

Do:

- Do have your attorney explain the types and natures of insurance policies involved.

- Do have your attorney explain whether and what insurance coverage is available and whether it is sufficient.

- Do choose a law firm with a proven track record in working with insurance coverage matters.

- Do give your attorney each and every policy you may have.

Don't:

- Don't decide what an insurance company's responsibility is. That is your lawyer's job.

- Don't decide which of your insurance policies apply to your case. Bring them all for your lawyer to sort through.

CHAPTER ELEVEN :
THE CASE IS FILED. NOW WHAT?

After you have danced through the steps of finding an attorney, hiring consultants and experts, investigating the defect to see if you actually have one, determining whether you potentially can recover, going through whatever pre-litigation procedures your state might require, and attempting to settle the matter, you finally file a lawsuit. What now?

First, you realize that with as much work, effort, and expense that is involved, it is doubtful that our nation is as litigious as people say. Who would want to go through all this for nothing? Then you realize the hard part has just begun.

Discovery

At the beginning of litigation, most attorneys design a discovery plan, which is a legal way of finding out the information the opposition may have. Since few construction defect cases actually go to trial, discovery is crucial in encouraging the other side to settle. Not only can a properly administered discovery process help guarantee trial success, it also will be integral to any settlement, arbitration, or mediation result.

Because construction defect cases are complicated, seldom is it enough to simply obtain information such as development and architectural plans, building specifications, government reports, governmental filings, cost estimates, and so forth, but it also is critical to obtain the necessary experts and consultants to analyze all that information.

A lawyer handling a construction defect case usually will ask the court to appoint a special referee familiar with this area of law and with the time available to handle discovery disputes. This greatly expedites the case and helps assure that discovery decisions remain fair and constant throughout the litigation.

While you will not necessarily be involved in the day-to-day aspects of discovery, your help will be needed in many aspects of discovery. Discovery involves requesting and producing documents, taking depositions, sending out subpoenas, interrogatories, and requests for admissions, and responding to the ones your attorney will receive from the defendants in your case. Therefore, you should have a basic understanding of the discovery process and the events that could occur.

Depositions: Tell Us What We Want to Know

In a deposition, a witness ("deponent") is questioned by one or more attorneys. While depositions usually take place in informal surroundings, they are taken as though they were conducted in court. The deponent is under oath. What the deponent says is taken down by a court reporter, and frequently videotaped.

Any party to the action can depose any other person, corporation, business, or government organization that may have information. For example, your attorney may want to depose the person who copied drawings within an architect's office to find out if there is a possibility your home's plans were intermixed with another architectural project.

Deposing a party to initiation only requires a notice to the party's attorney. Before a non-party can be deposed, he or she must be subpoenaed.

If you are to be deposed, your attorney most likely will want to meet with you to explain the nature and purpose of the deposition. You should understand that the range of questions during a deposition is very broad. During trial, only relevant questions can be asked. But during discovery proceedings, anything that can lead to relevant information is fair game as long as it is related to the subject of the lawsuit. The courts give considerable latitude to this.

In addition to requiring your presence, you may be obligated to bring records, files, or other evidence to the deposition. It is very important for you to discuss this with your lawyer to be sure you bring the correct documentation.

Admit This

You may be served a "Request for Admissions," which is a document asking you to admit or deny the genuineness of particular documents or the truth of specified matters of fact.

Interrogatories

Interrogatories are written questions, typically written in sets that one party asks another party. Generally they constitute an attempt to learn if you are the correct party, if your claim is justified, if your damages are justified, your background, and a wide assortment of specific details. Your attorney probably will send interrogatories to opposing parties to discover similar information.

The advantage of interrogatories is that they can ask for information on a wide variety of matters and can be used to nail down times, dates, names of parties, how the opposition plans to direct its case ("contentions interrogatories"), and to receive information that takes some research to obtain. They also are considerably less expensive than depositions because they do not require court reporters, video operators, travel expenses, or coffee and donuts for everyone.

There are disadvantages to interrogatories. They allow opposing parties to provide vague or evasive responses and the responding party cannot be prodded with immediate follow-up questions, nor can one deduce much about the demeanor or credibility of the witness. In addition, responses to interrogatories usually are prepared with the assistance of a lawyer. They lack spontaneity and rarely lead to great revelations.

Let Me See What You Have

Your lawyer may be served with, or may serve on the defendants, a "Request for Production and Inspection of Documents, Land, or Other Property." This is exactly what the name implies. Under your lawyer's guidance, you may assemble a great number of documents for the other side to view and copy in some manner. This can demand a lot of work on your part. It also can include any and all documents, photos, videos, recordings, computer disks, and other items in your files. The Requests for Production your lawyer serves on opposing counsel can result in file cabinets full of information. The information can include every drawing, plan, consumer contract, contractor and sub-contractor contracts, mortgage agreement, advertisement, brochure, memo, phone record, computer disk, photograph, video recording, and other type of documentation or record related in any way to the building of your home.

It is not unusual for attorneys involved in construction defect cases to have rooms full of file boxes for a single multi-million dollar case. This is one reason any lawyer you retain must have a capable staff of attorneys and paralegals. Someone must wade through all the records to reconstruct what actually happened in your case.

Besides documentation, you also may be requested to "produce" land or other property. This means you will have to make it available for thorough inspection. Since you are the one claiming a defect, it is only reasonable that you allow the opposing party to inspect the questioned property.

Requests for Production are extremely important, and you should work closely on them with your attorney. Preparing Requests for Production and responding to those requests are useful exercises, which help prepare you for depositions and trial, aid in drafting and responding to interrogatories, assist your expert consultants in their analyses, and facilitate organizing your case information.

Requests for Production can be served only by parties to the action on other parties to the lawsuit. Your lawyer will prepare subpoenas to obtain from non-parties documents and other things as potential evidence.

Disclose Your Experts

Opposing parties will want to know who your experts are, and you will want to know who their experts are. The law's disclosure requirement allows each side to depose the other's experts to discover their opinions and conclusions about your case. Some courts have very specific rules about when experts must be disclosed or lists of experts exchanged.

Defects, Truth, and Videotape

Frequently, attorneys videotape depositions. Video also is used extensively during property inspections, to record the nature and extent of damages for study during trial preparation and to demonstrate to the trial jury what the damages are.

Chapter Eleven Do's and Don'ts

Do:

- Do promptly provide whatever discovery information your attorney requests.

- Do meet with your attorney before you are deposed so he or she can explain the nature and purpose of the deposition.

- Give your lawyer all documents you were requested to produce for your deposition before the deposition so he or she can decide what is relevant and what should or should not be provided to the opposition.

Don't:

- Don't act slowly regarding discovery requests. There are time limits involved and missing them can harm your case.

- Don't withhold information from your attorney because you believe it is harmful to your case. That will cause more harm than good.

CHAPTER TWELVE:
STATUTE OF LIMITATIONS

The Bare Truth

One of the worst things that can happen to a plaintiff is to miss a statute of limitations time limit. These are legislative acts stating specific time periods one has to bring a lawsuit. The rationale behind them is that people, corporations, and other legal entities should not be forever liable for their acts and omissions. Over time, witnesses die or leave the area, memories fade, and documents get lost, all of which can make it difficult, if not impossible, to defend a lawsuit. In addition, it is thought that there should come a time when potential defendants (both criminal and civil) should no longer be under the threat of the continuing possibility of a lawsuit.

Not surprisingly, the construction, development and insurance industries seem to perpetually lobby legislative bodies to shorten these time limits. They argue that plaintiffs who know of a problem should not be allowed to sit on their rights for such a long period of time that it could place potential defendants at a serious disadvantage.

However, consumer groups argue that the industry simply desires to limit their liability by making it is as difficult as possible for a plaintiff to bring a lawsuit. Consumers may not even be aware of a defect—let alone of their right of a remedy—before the statute of limitations expires.

While courts enforce statutes of limitations, generally they abhor denying plaintiffs their day in court because of a legal technicality. Neither do courts, however, want plaintiffs—either because of ignorance, oversight, or simple tardiness—to be able to win lawsuits simply because vital evidence has disappeared.

Making the situation even more difficult, different jurisdictions can have very different statutes of limitations for the same cause of action, and different causes of action contained within the same lawsuit can have individual statutes of limitation. Also, the statutes of limitation are constantly changing. Prudent lawyers must be abreast of the latest changes, which is something most laypeople do not have the time or resources to do.

Not only is it difficult to determine when a statute of limitations has expired, it is equally as difficult to determine when the statute begins to run. In construction defect cases, the statutes generally begin upon "substantial completion" of the home (a phrase with a very technical and precise legal meaning, "substantial completion" is determined by a series of factors) or a "time of discovery" (also a very technical legal phrase, which usually is proven with evidence). The chief factor affecting the statute of limitations is whether the defect is patent or latent. Deciding the meaning of all these terms requires careful, close legal analysis and should be left to an attorney with considerable expertise in the area.

Another factor that can be involved is the concept of "repose," which is similar to a statute of limitations, but does not require a showing of knowledge. For example, a typical statute of limitations may say that a buyer has four years to file on a latent defect and three years on a patent defect, but in either case, the suit must be filed within ten years of "substantial completion." In this example, the ten-year period is a statute of repose.

It is vital to remember that the purpose of this book is not to provide legal advice and we strongly recommend you seek independent legal advice as soon as you suspect a construction defect to avoid losing your rights. However, we believe you should have a fundamental understanding of how these statutes operate and a basic education in how different states can—and do—set up statutory schemes. Therefore, we are providing an abbreviated explanation of several jurisdictions' statutes of limitations. It is critical you do not settle with this elementary explanation and that you consult a qualified attorney as soon as you get even the faintest whiff of a defect.

Different Strokes for Different States

California Limits

In California, the general rule is that in construction defect claims the statute of limitations is four years for patent (obvious) defects or three years from the date of discovery for latent (hidden) defects, with an outside limit of ten years from the date of substantial completion—called a statute of "repose."

The California rule has numerous pitfalls. First, a decision must be made as to whether a defect is latent or patent. Next, if the defect is latent, the time of discovery must be determined. Consumers should be wary of developers who have been known to send people out to ask homeowner association members when they first noticed a defect. If the association has hundreds of members, the developer may find one homeowner claiming to have known of the problem for years, even if he or she has no idea a problem existed or what caused the problem. For this and other reasons, homeowners should not speak to anyone other than representatives of their lawyer's firm or homeowner association.

Where the Chips Fall in Nevada

In Nevada, you have six, eight or ten years, depending on the circumstances. Nevada's statute of limitations is slightly more complex and involves more factors than California's. Basically, it consists of four parts:

1. An action based on willful misconduct may be brought any time after substantial completion.

2. Actions based on defects known to the builder may be brought within ten years from substantial completion.

3. Actions based on latent defects (not apparent by reasonable inspection) may be brought within eight years after substantial completion.

4. Actions based on patent defects (apparent by reasonable inspection) may be brought within six years after substantial completion.

Arizona's Gritty Truth

The Arizona statute is dependent upon the cause of action in which a plaintiff sues. (See generally Chapter Nine for information on causes of action.)

For breach of implied warranty and habitability, the plaintiff has six years to bring the action from the date of discovery. If the plaintiff brings the action under negligence, there is a two-year statute, but that does not apply to personal injury or damage to personal property.

Arizona also has other limitations. Actions brought in contract, which includes implied warranties, must be brought within eight years from substantial completion unless the damage occurs within the eighth year, in which case the statute is extended for one year. This is another outside limit, regardless of the date of discovery.

How Long Sun Shines on your Cause of Action in Florida

Florida law provides home purchasers a legislated warranty of up to five years, depending upon what is damaged, the type of damages and the amount of time that has passed since certain events.

Florida makes a distinction between "improvements to real property" and condominiums and provides separate statutes as to each.

In an action regarding improvements to real property, the buyer has four years except for an action on latent defects, in which case the action must be brought at no time later than fifteen years from completion or from a long list of other assorted criteria such as the date of possession by owner or the date a certificate of occupancy was issued.

It is important to note that the date of completion can be very complex, and Florida law provides a wide array of possibilities.

For condominiums, there is an implied warranty of habitability and fitness for a particular use for three years from the time of completion. For personal property, such as ranges or refrigerators, the owner has the length of the manufacturer's warranty. However, for roofs and other structural elements, there is a three-year statute or one year after owners other than the developer have taken possession, not to exceed five years.

Untangling this mess can be an onerous task and requires analysis by a skilled attorney.

The Texas Two-Step

In Texas, an outside limit on a builder's or contractor's liability is ten years, which may be extended two extra years if the damages occur in the tenth year and a written damages claim is presented to potential defendants.

Things in Texas get stickier, yet. Under certain theories of liability, the buyer has only four years from the time of discovery, while under another cause of action, such as Deceptive Trade Practices, the plaintiff may be limited to two years. Warning: The Texas statutes also can turn on many other factors. If you even suspect a defect, see an attorney.

Illinois' Midwestern Sensibility

Illinois plaintiffs can bring suit up to four years from the time they knew or should have known of the defect. However, the action must be brought within ten years of the date the home was substantially completed unless the defect is discovered within the ten-year limit but the four-year term has not yet run, in which case the four-year limit will be allowed to run even if it exceeds the ten year limit.

After reading this, you should understand two things: 1) why lawyers think like they do, and 2) that you should (especially in Illinois) retain a lawyer as soon as you suspect a construction defect.

So far, it may seem straightforward enough, but don't be deceived. Little in the law is simple (see the previous two paragraphs). Deciding when substantial completion occurs is a matter of debate.

Lawyers can spend what seems like a lifetime arguing whether a defect is patent or latent. Different causes of action can have different statutes of limitations and different time periods of repose. The difference between the applicable statutes of limitation and time periods of repose is a technical analysis your lawyer will need to make after reviewing the relevant statutes and case law.

Chapter Twelve Do's and Don'ts

Do:

- To avoid losing your rights, seek independent legal advice as soon as you suspect a construction defect.

- If you have had an expert, contractor or home inspector look at your home and provide a report, your statute may be running. You can protect the privacy of this information by having the expert and his or her report sent to your lawyer when it is complete.

Don't:

- Don't try to figure out for yourself whether the statute of limitations or period of repose has run. Leave that to your attorney.

- Don't turn over an expert or contractor's report or repair estimate to a developer. It may trigger a statute of limitations.

CHAPTER THIRTEEN: DAMAGES

In legalese, "damages" usually means "money." The general purpose of damages is to make the injured party "whole" again, or to return the party to its position before the injury or loss. "Punitive damages" is money intended to punish the offender by making the offender pay more than the amount of actual damages for particularly offensive behavior. Either way, the success or failure of a case can hinge on damages awards and the availability of funds to pay those damages.

Whether or not a particular type of damage can be recovered varies from state to state. In some states, damages that may occur in the future, such as from a potential earthquake, can be recovered in some jurisdictions.

Diminution of Value Versus Cost of Repairs

Plaintiffs in construction defect complaints usually request either "diminution of value" or "cost of repairs" damages. The former usually is used when repair is not possible or the value of the house is reduced because of the fact that it has any sort of defect. For example, suppose your home is built near an earthquake fault, and the existence of the fault causes a reduction in your home's value. If the value of your house new was $200,000, and later you discover the nearby earthquake fault which the developer either knew about or should have known about, the value of your home could be reduced by half. This loss of $100,000 has to be made up to you from somewhere.

Typically, the cost of repair is the right damage calculation and is used in 95 percent of cases. However, if you sell your home you may lose your right to collect these damages on single-family structures.

Stigma—Or, If It Happened Before, It Could Happen Again

Suppose repairs are made, but your home still is reduced in value because a potential buyer is fearful that the injury, such as a landslide or earthquake, could recur? This is referred to as a "stigma" on the property. Some courts will allow recovery for it. Recent case law, however, has limited stigma damages to catastrophic problems such as landslides or earthquakes.

The balance between diminution of value and repair costs is a delicate one and seemingly always in a state of evolution. For instance, in diminution of value cases, often the homeowner wants to move and purchase a home with no defects. Moving and related costs may be recoverable along with fluxuations in interest rates and property taxes. Again, however, damage calculations are extremely complicated and usually are arrived at with the aid of many experts.

Attorney Fees

Attorney fees usually are not recoverable in California, but they are in other states such as Arizona and Nevada.

Expert Fees and Costs

The prevailing party in a construction defect case frequently will recover expert fees and related costs. Because of the complexity of construction defect cases, these fees and costs can be considerable.

Punitive Damages

Courts do not like to allow punitive damages. In California, plaintiffs must show by clear and convincing evidence that the defendant was guilty of fraud, malice, or oppression. Other states have different standards for punitive damages.

In California, an advantage of receiving punitive damages, besides the extra compensation, is that sometimes the plaintiff then will be able to recover attorney fees.

Chapter Thirteen Do's and Don'ts

Do:

- Do help your attorney prepare as quickly and effectively as possible.

- Do have your attorney explain all potential settlement possibilities and methods.

Don't:

- Don't attempt to calculate the value of your damages. That's your expert's job.

- Don't hesitate to tell your expert or your attorney of any potential damages.

CHAPTER FOURTEEN:
WHO WANTS TO GO TO COURT?

Nearly 95 percent of construction defect cases never go to trial. Almost always, parties to a defect case would rather settle, mediate, or arbitrate the case than go to trial. Taking a case to trial always has risks. For plaintiffs, there is always the chance a verdict or judgment will be well below what is needed for repair, and for defendants the possibility of an unexpectedly large award looms. In short, jury decisions are extremely hard to predict. As a result, every potential party should have a familiarity with how cases are resolved before trial.

Settlement Strategies

Consumers should have a rudimentary understanding of what can encourage an early settlement in order to help their lawyers quickly resolve their cases. Early preparation is the single most important factor in getting a case to early settlement. This means getting your experts together as soon as possible, having damage reports, repair estimates, and other settlement requirements completed, conducting discovery, and creating settlement strategies. Only then can one make the subtlest of settlement overtures.

An experienced lawyer will know how to organize everyone to possibly reach an early settlement. However, it is doubtful the opposing party will settle unless a trial date is set, and this cannot be done until your case is properly prepared. Without an early trial date, the chance of an early settlement diminishes rapidly.

Your attorney can control the pace of the trial, but defense counsel will frequently attempt to slow the process. Defendants frequently believe the longer they can prolong the case, the more eager the plaintiffs will be to settle the case for a lower amount. Frequently, defense attorneys attempt to slow down the process by bringing in new possible defendants such as subcontractors and design professionals. A skilled plaintiff's attorney can circumvent this, or at least lessen the impact, by settling with some defendants who then can ask for reimbursement from some or all of the remaining defendants.

If the defense is quickly forced to trial, they will be fearful of a large jury award and will be less likely to be properly prepared for trial. Look at it as a football game: The offense wants to get a touchdown as quickly as possible, the defense wants to eat up as much time as possible to prevent the touchdown. It is only when you are in a scoring position that the opposition will be ready to discuss settlement.

You must, therefore, work as closely as possible with your attorney to prepare the case as quickly as possible. Or, as a famous Civil War general once said, the winner is the one "who gets there firstest with the mostest."

Your attorney's job is to organize the offense and to educate the opposition to the strength of your case. If you and your lawyer present a persuasive argument and it becomes apparent you have a winning case, the question is not if the case will settle, but what the settlement will be.

Jointly Retained Experts

Often, once settlement begins, the primary dispute is either the amount of settlement or the type and scope of anticipated repairs. The result can be an impasse with neither side willing to budge, particularly if the sides are too far apart.

The parties can overcome that standoff by appointing joint experts to review the paperwork, plans, specifications, soils reports, and any other relevant documentation involved. Both plaintiffs and defendants participate in the selection process.

It is important to both sides of the action that they choose experts who have neither strong plaintiff nor defense bias. If the expert's opinion on repairs and necessary costs obviously favors one party, it is doubtful the expert will be acceptable to all parties.

Usually, using jointly retained experts happens only in the early stages of litigation and requires that all the parties trust each other to live up to whatever agreement they entered into. This agreement, of course, should be in writing.

Large Developers Who Want to Keep Their Reputations

Large reputable developers find it in their self-interest to maintain consumer goodwill and their own good name. These desires enter into settlement negotiations in two ways. First, in projects that are sold in phases, the State Department of Real Estate from states such as California, Arizona, and Nevada can review a developer's alleged misrepresentation in completed housing phases to see if there could be a pattern of misrepresentation stretching to uncompleted phases. In addition, when a developer submits a subdivision approval application, the developer must guarantee that no known defects exist and that when the homes are sold, no misrepresentations to consumers will be made. If a defect exists, after an investigation the Department of Real Estate may stop construction and sale of future stages. Then, the developer may have to make significant changes in the design or construction technique. This could cause considerable loss of time and money by the developer.

The second way reputation enters in settlement is simply the overall loss of reputation and strain on resources a lawsuit can cause. If it is apparent, especially early in litigation, that there is a defect and most likely the developer eventually will lose in court, settlement will save a lot of trouble. In these types of settlements, the developers usually require that individual homeowners keep the settlement terms confidential. This allows the developers both to settle with different homeowners for different amounts and keep their good reputation intact.

Homeowner Association Settlements

Depending on how property is held, homeowner associations frequently have the power to settle the claim. In this case, homeowners and their association's board of directors must work closely together to assure all homeowners receive a just settlement.

Less frequently, homeowners and their associations have conflicts of interest. In those cases, each entity will have separate attorneys. This helps eliminate potential conflicts.

Cash or Carry?

Monetary settlements are not the only settlement possibility. Fairly sophisticated methods can be employed. The developer can offer replacement property of equivalent value and guarantee the same monthly payment, number of payments, and interest. There are disadvantages to this settlement method. First, it may require a move to a different neighborhood and a change of schools, and new friends for you and your children. Next, a move of only a block or two can influence how quickly or slowly the new property appreciates. It also requires moving a household, which can be a stressful and expensive process.

Another settlement alternative is for the developer to agree to pay money over time, usually by purchasing an annuity. This is especially useful if defects are anticipated in the future because of design or construction problems.

Settling claims of individual defects separately sometimes is a useful settlement strategy. Some claims, such as leaky roofs, require quick repair. Others, such as land subsidence or structural problems, can be settled at a later time. This allows the developer to quickly settle claims believed to be legitimate, and also helps the homeowners repair particular defects quickly and efficiently.

Getting It All Down

Settlement terms are always reduced to writing, and a request to dismiss any lawsuit is filed with the court. The settlement terms are then incorporated into a release that is signed by all of the parties agreeing to the settlement.

One type of release, called a general release, should be entered into with caution. A general release frees defendants from all liability for any past, present and future liability. There could be undiscovered defects for which the developer will be escaping liability. Astute plaintiffs' attorneys will restrict the release to known and specified defects. You should be sure your attorney explains to you all the terms of any release you consider signing. Among the questions you should ask your lawyer are:

- Who does the release cover?
- What defects does the release cover?
- When does the release go into effect?
- How does the release cover unknown damages?

If the release does cover undiscovered or future defects (a general release), why should I sign it?

Sometimes a general release is the only viable option, and if your experts have carefully investigated the property to assure you no other defects exist or are expected, signing a general release may be reasonable.

The Enforcer

Settlement agreements should contain provisions to enforce the settlement terms and to allow the court in which the case is brought to retain jurisdiction, and therefore the authority, to enforce the settlement. In most states, the parties will want to place any agreement into the trial court record in case of future patented problems. Generally, settlements are enforced as contracts, but if it is a court order, the party or party's attorney violating the settlement could be held in contempt of court and have sanctions imposed.

Homeowner Association Rules

Many states require homeowner associations to follow special procedures when settling a lawsuit. Even if the state has no requirements, the CC&Rs may dictate how the settlement must be handled. At the very least, the board of directors, if not the entire membership, should approve the agreement.

California law requires disclosure to homeowner association members of defects not repaired at the time a case is settled. The law covers defects in common interest portions of the property and defects in private interest portions that the association has a duty to maintain and repair.

Among the items which must be disclosed in California are:

- A good faith estimate, at the time of disclosure, of when the association believes the repairs will be made
- A list of the defects that are not included in the estimated plan for repairs, and what the status is of each of those defects

Alternative Dispute Resolution

Recent years have seen clogged court calendars, a rise in expensive and time-consuming pretrial discovery, an increase in pretrial motions and legal maneuvering. This can cause the expenses to balloon, and it can take years to get a case to trial. It also means more and more cases are decided on narrow legal issues often full of procedural problems.

When the consumer actually gets his or her day in court, the issues can be too complex for most juries and judges to understand. Judges, who seldom have a construction defect litigation background, must be brought up to speed. Juries, usually consisting of average citizens, often have an even bigger challenge trying to understand these cases.

Many litigants, unhappy with the current legal system, have turned to Alternate Dispute Resolution (ADR), which can quickly, fairly, and economically resolve the cases outside the judicial system. ADR also allows the parties to solve their disputes amicably. Developers, after all, are in business to build homes, not to be involved in litigation, and homeowners want to continue their lives without the stress of lawsuits hanging over their heads.

ADR provides many types of formats as alternatives to trial. Mediation, arbitration, the use of retired judges or impartial disinterested attorneys, and voluntary settlement conferences are among the more popular methods for dispute resolution. Usually there are costs involved. Lawyers and other professional mediation services must be paid. A retired judge (sometimes referred to as "rent-a-judge") also must be paid. Customarily, these costs are split among the parties. Also, court evidence rules can be arbitrary and prevent some information from reaching the jury. ADR is much more informal and allows the parties to plead their cases with fewer restrictions. You should have a general idea of what these ADR settlement methods are so when attorneys toss these terms around you will know what you are paying for.

Mediation

This is a non-binding process where the mediator attempts to bring the parties to an agreement. The parties retain the right to accept or reject the settlement offers. Mediators vary in their persuasive abilities, and some parties are more eager to settle than others. Commonly, mediation is used as a last effort before arbitration or trial, and generally occurs in a casual environment with both lawyers and parties present.

Arbitration

Sometimes after a defect is discovered or, often, when a home is purchased, the parties agree to arbitrate any disputes. Arbitration has rules similar to court rules, but generally they are slightly less rigid and more open to interpretation.

There are two types of arbitration. In "binding" arbitration, you are pretty much stuck with the ruling. In "non-binding" arbitration, the rulings can be rejected and taken to court.

Voluntary Settlement Conferences

Most courts require mandatory settlement conferences before trial. Many courts allow, and even encourage, voluntary settlement conferences. These are very similar to mediation. The parties agree on the rules, retain a retired jurist or other trusted person to preside, and proceed.

Usually, the settlement judge listens to each side and then gives his opinion of how a judge and jury would rule.

General Reference

The parties may agree to enter into a procedure called "general reference," which is an agreement to decide certain issues—lawyers learn in law school how to spot issues—by asking the court to appoint a referee to rule on particular questions. These rulings and findings by the referee are unchangeable at trial.

In general reference, the parties also can reserve certain issues to be ruled on in court. This can save considerable time and money by shortening the time attorneys and experts spend in trial.

Chapter Fourteen Do's and Don'ts

Do:

- Consider alternate settlement strategies and discuss them with your lawyer.

- Remember that defendants have just as much to lose from a jury verdict as you do.

- Realize that defendants may be as eager to enter into alternate settlement strategies as you are.

- Discuss any release of liability with your attorney very carefully.

Don't:

- Don't be surprised if your case never makes it to trial. Ninety-five percent of all cases settle.

- Don't forget to provide as much help as you can to your attorney. Early preparation encourages early and successful settlement.

- Don't enter into settlement negotiations without your attorney.

CHAPTER FIFTEEN:
CONCLUSION — OR,
THE STORY CONTINUES

If you have made it this far, congratulations. We hope you see what a long trip construction defect claims can be. If you are unable to obtain an early settlement or negotiate with your builder before bringing litigation, perhaps we have helped you understand why lawyers jump through seemingly dozens of legal hoops bringing a construction defect claim. If you want a truer taste of a defect case, take a look at the construction defect textbook we wrote for other lawyers, *Handling Construction Defect Claims: Western States.*

Unfortunately, lawyers and courts are forced by the facts of each case and the necessary elasticity of the laws to raise the suitably simple to the height of the incredibly complex. In short, Ockham's Razor, the logic premise that says the simplest answer is always the best answer, may apply in philosophy, but seems to be useless in litigation. Why?

Partly, it is because lawyers enjoy seeing both subtlety and complexity. Partly, it is because of the linguistic development of the words lawyers use. To paraphrase Strunk and White's *Elements of Style*, we tend to be drawn to five-dollar Latin-based verbiage to express half-dollar ideas because historically the educated in our culture spoke and wrote in Latin or Greek, even though the people spoke in English. Mostly, however, it is because the legal principles must be applied to a virtually infinite number of fact situations and constantly changing societal and social needs. Almost always, lawyers learn intellectual purity in law school, only to discover after graduation that few cases even remotely resemble the ones they studied.

Practicing law is like playing a baseball game where the batter is seldom presented with a simple fastball. Instead, lawyers are almost always thrown curves, sliders, change-ups, knuckleballs, and the occasional screwball for confusion.

We can see this by examining the development of construction defect law. Originally, the homebuyers would go to a craftsman builder, tell him what they wanted, then wait and watch while the house was built. These charming houses, discernible by their attention to detail, hardwood floors, and plaster interior walls, make up neighborhoods in every city in America.

If one of these houses was poorly built, the consumer sued the builder under the law of contracts. He would tell the court that he agreed to give the builder money in exchange for the builder constructing a home. The buyer would say that they had a contract and that the builder breached that contract. The buyer, however, was stuck with the theory of *caveat emptor.*

What happened if the house was built, but not built as well as should be? The buyer could claim that the builder was negligent. The contractor had a duty to build a decent house, and in some important way he breached that duty. For example, the builder may have had a duty to use decent cured lumber but instead, to save a few dollars, used green lumber, which cracked under the building's weight. Pretty simple, right? Ah, but now come the curve balls. What if the person stuck with the faulty housing is not the original buyer? What if a builder can't be shown to be negligent in a particular way, but the house is defective anyway?

After World War II, housing began to be mass produced, just like cars and table saws. Custom-built homes became a privilege of the rich or, occasionally, the merely eccentric. (One person we know built his home in a tree, another dug a hole in the ground and kept digging until he dug the rooms for his home, and another built walls for his home out of the rocks he found in nearby canyons.) Tract housing made for instant neighborhoods. Next came planned unit developments, which owned the communal roadways, swimming pools, spas and other amenities. Apartment-style condominiums, where the homeowner associations own the entire unit, then became common. These new housing types presented new and challenging issues for consumers, lawyers, and courts.

New building techniques also created problems. Understanding these new construction methods required lawyers and courts to expand their areas of expertise.

Housing was being built on hillsides and in valleys that either were carved out of land previously too steep to be built upon, or on fill materials used to level canyons and arroyos. Suddenly, geotechnical and civil engineers became required for many claims and created additional litigation expenses.

Also, builders started using space-age building methods and materials, which caused environmental and other problems. New roofing materials and other coverings created water-intrusion problems that resulted in mold, mildew, and rot. These problems meant the law had to be redesigned and restructured as well. Legal principles were expanded from contract law all the way to strict liability.

Construction defect law still is expanding and evolving. Within a year or two this book will have to be updated. Under pressure from insurance companies over the last decade, the legislatures in many states have spent considerable time and effort re-evaluating the entire American tort system. It seems during every election, our courts are under fire from all directions by well-funded industry groups who either want to significantly limit or even eliminate consumers' rights to redress.

Of course, limiting Americans' rights to gain access to our legal system would be disastrous to consumer rights. Homebuyers will be prey to unethical developers who seek to increase profits to the detriment of consumers. (See Appendix E.)

Such limitations eventually would affect other consumer protections. People injured by dangerous products or poisonous medications, or have consumed tainted foods, might lose access to legal redress. Also, victims of drunk drivers and other types of automobile accidents may be forced to endure lifetime problems, and many other injured defendants may be prevented from receiving compensation.

Luckily, our judicial system has stood firm against the onslaughts, primarily because the American voter has a deep and abiding belief in fair play. Because of this belief, when new homebuyers invest their life savings in new homes, they can get what they pay for.

APPENDIX

APPENDIX A

Do's and Don'ts

APPENDIX B

Attorney Hiring Checklist

APPENDIX C

The Twelve Most Commonly Asked Questions

APPENDIX D

Eleven Builders' Myths

APPENDIX E

Top 15 Reasons Why Builders Face Construction Defects Lawsuits

APPENDIX A: DO'S AND DON'TS

Even though each of these Do's and Don'ts have appeared at the end of each relevant chapter, we have grouped them together here as an aid to the reader and for easy reference.

Chapter One Do's and Don'ts

Do:

- Do be on the lookout for defects when inspecting the property for purchase.

- Do remember defects can result from dozens of design and construction problems.

- Do retain an independent and qualified home inspector before purchasing property.

- Do read any builder warranty carefully. You'll be surprised what it does not cover.

Don't:

- Don't take the developers word for construction quality.

- Don't be talked into a false sense of security by clever developers and brokers.

- Don't forget to notify your homeowner association of potential defects.

Chapter Two Do's and Don'ts

Do:

- Do have your lawyer explain to you in simple and clear terms the type and nature of any defect.

- Do notify your lawyer and homeowner association of any suspected defect. What appears at first to be a minor problem could develop into a catastrophic one.

- Do remember that not all defects can be easily seen. Some are hidden behind walls and under slabs.

- Do carefully maintain your property. Perform an annual checkup.

- Do remember that many people and entities are potential defendants. Don't release anyone without consulting an attorney.

Don't:

- Don't assume that just because a defect can't be seen that one does not exist. For example, excessive creaking, mold, or unpleasant odors can be signs of defects.

- Don't attempt to analyze potential defects. That is your lawyer's and expert's job.

- Don't hesitate to inform your lawyer or homeowner association of potential defects. Because of complex statute of limitations, if you snooze, you could lose.

Chapter Three Do's and Don'ts

Do:

- Do always hire your experts and consultants through your attorney. Otherwise, you could lose confidentiality.

- Do give your attorney any and all documentation that may be even remotely related to a defect.

- Do familiarize yourself to the number and types of experts that may be required.

- Do promptly fill out and respond to any forms or surveys your attorney or experts may send you.

- Do familiarize yourself with your maintenance responsibilities and the responsibilities of your homeowner association. Read your CC&R's (Covenants Conditions and Restrictions).

Don't:

- Don't forget you may be responsible for your expert's fees and costs. Get a preliminary estimate before you start.

- Don't attempt to analyze the nature and cause of your problems yourself. This is why experts are hired.

Chapter Four Do's and Don'ts

Do:

- Do have your attorney examine your Covenants, Conditions and Restrictions if there is a question whether your homeowner association should be notified.

- Do be familiar with potential defects. Among the categories are: leaking windows, doors and roofs, exterior stucco and siding defects, improper drainage, design defects, poor materials selection, faculty construction techniques, mold and mildew, and faulty mass-produced items.

Don't:

- Don't tell the developer of a defect unless your attorney directs you to do so.

- Don't let the developer make "Band-Aid" repairs. The defects will reappear next year.

Chapter Five Do's and Don'ts

Do:

- Do meet with several law firms and obtain separate proposals from each.

- Do evaluate and review a law firm's basic knowledge and experience with construction defect cases, trial and mediation experience, track record, settlement history, reputation, integrity, fees, and advancing expert costs.

- Do tell your attorney of all potential plaintiffs and defendants so he or she can check for conflicts of interest.

- Do check references.

- Do check to see if the potential law firm is large enough and has the staff resources and finances to effectively pursue the claim.

- Do establish a protocol to efficiently and effectively communicate with your attorney to maintain confidentiality.

- Do maintain a separate file for each homeowner if multiple home-owners are pursuing claims.

- Do carefully negotiate fees.

- Do make sure the fee agreement makes allowances for alternate settlement methods such as buy backs and developer-conducted repairs.

Don't:

- Don't hesitate to have a second attorney give an opinion, even if your attorney has already made a claim or filed suit.

- Don't hire an attorney who is a homeowner or association member.

- Don't hire the association's corporate or general counsel law firm to pursue a construction defect claim.

- Don't hire an attorney just because he or she has a close personal relationship with a board member.

- Don't limit yourself by not considering a change of attorneys if you are not satisfied with your current attorney.

Chapter Six Do's and Don'ts

Do:

- Do have your attorney ascertain if the developer has assets or insurance to pay a claim.

- Do have your attorney explain the various methods of financing a lawsuit.

Don't:

- Don't proceed without carefully analyzing all litigation costs.

Chapter Seven Do's and Don'ts

Do:

- Do carefully explain to potential buyers if you are in the middle of a defect dispute, and who will receive any recovery. Put such information in the purchase agreement.

- Do have your attorney decide if the homeowner association, individual homeowners or both should bring suit.

- Do understand that the term "Homeowner Association" can include many different ownership entities such as Common Interest Development, Condominiums, Townhomes, and Homeowner Associations that own common areas.

- Do have your attorney explain what individual homeowners own and what the homeowner association owns.

Don't:

- Don't fail to carefully explain to potential buyers if you are in the middle of a defect dispute and who will receive any recovery. Put such information in the purchase agreement.

Chapter Eight Do's and Don'ts

Do:

- Do promptly provide any information your lawyer needs to complete any statutorily required pre-litigation steps.

- Do familiarize yourself with whatever pre-litigating steps your jurisdiction may have.

- Do act promptly. Many states have complex time limits on pre-litigation steps.

Don't:

- Don't act slowly. You must meet the deadlines, or you could lose your right to your claim.

- Don't believe the builder has your interests in mind.

Chapter Nine Do's and Don'ts

Do:

- Do learn some of the important terminology that applies to your case.

Don't:

- Don't be embarrassed to ask your lawyer questions if you don't understand something about your case.

Chapter Ten Do's and Don'ts

Do:

- Do have your attorney explain the types and nature of insurance policies involved.

- Do have your attorney explain what insurance coverage is available and whether it is sufficient.

- Do choose a law firm with a proven track record on recovering from developer insurance policies.

- Do give your attorney each and every policy you may have.

Don't:

- Don't decide what an insurance company's responsibility is. That is your lawyer's job.

Chapter Eleven Do's and Don'ts

Do:

- Do promptly provide whatever discovery information your attorney requests.

- Do meet with your attorney before you are deposed so he or she can explain the nature and purpose of the deposition.

- Do give your lawyer all documents requested for your deposition before the deposition so he or she can decide what is relevant and what should or shouldn't be provided to the opposition.

Don't:

- Don't act slowly regarding discovery requests. There are time limits involved and missing them can harm your case.

- Don't withhold information because you believe it is harmful to your case. That will cause more harm than good.

Chapter Twelve Do's and Don'ts

Do:

- To avoid losing your rights, do seek independent legal advice as soon as you suspect a construction defect.

Don't:

- Don't try to figure out for yourself whether the statute of limitations or period of repose has run. Leave that to your attorney.

Chapter Thirteen Do's and Don'ts

Do:

- Do help your attorney prepare as quickly and effectively as possible.

- Do have your attorney explain all potential settlement possibilities and methods.

Don't:

- Don't attempt to calculate the value of your damages. That's your expert's job.

- Don't hesitate to tell your expert or your attorney of any potential damages.

Chapter Fourteen Do's and Don'ts

Do:

- Consider alternate settlement strategies and discuss them with your lawyer.

- Remember that defendants have just as much to lose from a jury verdict as you do.

- Realize that defendants may be as eager to enter into alternate settlement strategies as you are.

- Discuss any release of liability with your attorney very carefully.

Don't:

- Don't be surprised if your case never makes it to trial. Ninety-five percent of all cases settle.

- Don't forget to provide as much help as you can to your attorney. Early preparation encourages early and successful settlement.

- Don't enter into settlement negotiations without your attorney.

APPENDIX B:
ATTORNEY HIRING CHECKLIST

BOARD OF DIRECTORS ATTORNEY SELECTION CRITERIA

SELECTION CRITERIA	FIRM X	FIRM Y
1. Practice exclusively construction defect litigation; no HOA general counsel work, no developer work.	_____	_____
2. A significant track record of substantial recoveries.	_____	_____
3. 60 Day Program/case evaluation/due diligence without charge.	_____	_____
4. Ability to finance expert investigation.	_____	_____
5. Capability of handling a case on contingency-staying power.	_____	_____
6. Strong background of having worked for developers and their insurance companies.	_____	_____
7. A solid reputation and credibility with the opposition.	_____	_____
8. Ability to work effectively with experts to identify all major defects.	_____	_____
9. Trained staff of attorneys and paralegals, well versed in construction defect litigation.	_____	_____
10. Local counsel affiliation to service your needs.	_____	_____

APPENDIX C: TWELVE MOST ASKED QUESTIONS AND ANSWERS

The following questions are designed to offer broad information for various topics in construction defects. Most of what is discussed here is developed further in various parts of this book.

1. What is a construction defect?

Almost any condition that reduces the value of a home, condominium, or common area can be legally recognized as a *defect in design or workmanship*, or a *defect related to land movement*. Courts throughout the United States have recognized two primary categories of defects for which damages are recoverable by the homeowner or homeowner association.

Defects in design, workmanship and materials: These include dry rot; water seepage through roofs windows and sliding glass doors; siding and stucco deficiencies; slab leaks or cracks; faulty drainage; improper landscaping and irrigation; termite infestation; improper materials; structural failure or collapse; defective plumbing; faulty electrical wiring; inadequate environmental controls; defective lighting or security; insufficient insulation and poor sound protection; and absence of firewalls.

Landslide and earth settlement problems: Examples are expansive soils; underground water or streams; ancient landslides; vertical settlement; horizontal movement; land sloughing or sliding; improper compaction; inadequate grading; and drainage. Structural failures and earth movement conditions can be catastrophic in nature and present both personal injury and substantial property damage exposure. Landslide and settlement conditions may result in collapse of roofs; cracks in slabs, walls, foundations, and ceilings; disturbance of public or private utilities; and sometimes a complete undermining of the structures.

2. What does the builder's warranty really cover?

Read the warranty carefully. Every warranty is different in what is covered and what is not, how long the warranty lasts, and what the builder will do to fix construction problems. Most will not address eighty percent of typical construction defects. Many require you to arbitrate and give up your right to sue in court. You also may end up paying the developer's arbitration costs if you lose. Do not be duped into believing they will repair defects to your satisfaction. The warranty is more a marketing tool than any real effort to address serious problems in your home, and most developers' concept of what constitutes a construction defect falls far short of what most building experts, applying contemporary building standards, say is a construction defect.

3. How do I prove that a defect exists?

In most cases, you will need to hire the services of an expert. Experts are those who have the necessary training, education and experience to give testimony in court as to the cause of a defect. For example, if your roof leaks, a waterproofing expert who has designed effective roofs, evaluated other defective leaky roofs and knows how roofs should be built would be in a good position to testify on why your roof leaks. And while a general or roofing contractor can repair a damaged roof, he may not be the best person to act as your expert. Your lawyer cannot, in most cases, prove his case against the developer unless he has a qualified expert. Experts are available in nearly every aspect of residential construction. An expert's services usually run from $125.00 to $250.00 or more per hour.

4. What kinds of damages can I recover in a lawsuit, and can I recover attorney's fees?

All courts are clear in awarding condominium owners' associations the cost of repairing the defects. You can also recover whatever reasonable fees you have had to pay for your experts to investigate the cause of your defects and their costs in supervising the repairs. The costs of doing temporary repairs during and before the lawsuit to prevent further the damage are also recoverable. If repairs require owners to vacate their homes, these relocation costs are included. Punitive damages, or damages awarded to punish the developer and to deter similar conduct in the future, may be awarded where the developer defendant has defrauded the buyer. With few exceptions, attorney's fees are generally not recoverable but are negotiated as a part of any settlement.

5. What should I do if the developer has agreed to make the necessary repairs?

It is wise to consult an experienced lawyer who can assist in locating an independent expert (one who has no relationship with the developer) to evaluate the developer's investigation of the problem and his proposed repair. The same expert should oversee actual repairs. Once repairs are agreed upon, the attorney can draft a proper settlement agreement that does not release the developer of liability except for the limited and defined repairs being made, and then only after the repairs have proved effective. The developer typically demands a broad form general release of all future liability in exchange for making repairs. Such a release may result in board of director liability and eliminate your right to sue for other defects that appear during the time remaining on your statutes of limitation. For that reason such a release is rarely, if ever, recommended. In other words, insist on a specific limited release.

6. How long do I have to file a lawsuit?

All construction defect cases are covered by statutes of limitation. One statute requires the homeowner association to file suit within six, eight or ten years from the time of substantial completion of each development phase. Another (California's) requires suit within ten years for hidden defects and four years for obvious defects. Arizona's three-year statute of limitations for statutory warranty claims starts to tick away as soon as the development ownership transitions to individual homeowners. Under another statute, you are required to file within three years from the time you first discovered each defect. Under the three-year rule, courts are not too rigid on when "discovery" of a defect occurs. Generally, the defect must be of such a magnitude that a reasonable person should have discovered it. However, letters to the developer, surveys of homeowners' complaints, boards of directors' minutes, committee reports, reserve studies and experts' reports may prove a defect has been discovered. Upon discovery of the defect, take prompt, appropriate action to protect your rights. By all means, before you start your lawsuit, get it in writing from your lawyer that none of these time limits have been blown. Don't try to analyze statute of limitations legal issues. They are very complex and require expert legal opinion.

7. How much will a lawsuit cost?

The total cost of prosecuting a lawsuit will depend on a number of factors, including the nature and amount of damages, the number of parties, and the attitude of the parties. Some lawsuits are settled within a relatively short period of time, while others are not resolved until just before trial. Lawsuits can be expensive, and close cooperation between homeowners, the homeowner association, property manager and attorney is necessary to contain the costs as much as possible. One of the major costs is the cost of expert consultants; these costs are usually included in the lawsuit. Experts' costs will depend upon the nature and extent of defects and the size of the project. Attorneys generally either bill by the hour or take a percentage of any recovery. If the attorney charges by the hour, expect to pay between $200 and $300 or more per hour for one with experience. If the attorney works on a contingency basis, expect the fee to be between 28% and 38% of the gross recovery. These fees are always negotiable. Whatever the agreement, get it in writing. Most owners prefer the attorney to take the risk and ask for a contingency contract. Under a contingency agreement, if you don't get paid, your lawyer doesn't get paid.

8. Where do I get the money to pay for a lawsuit?

If your property has a homeowner association, several ways exist to raise money for pursuing your legal rights. First, your association's reserves are a good source. Many states allow associations to borrow for reserves as long as it is paid pack in a limited amount of time. Another source is to increase your monthly assessments by the percentage allowed in your CC&Rs or pass a special assessment. Finally, certain lenders will finance the investigation, securing the loan with the potential recovery. You also can ask your lawyer to advance expenses. In a class action, these costs are split among all the participants. The larger the group of homeowners, the less you will be responsible to pay in costs.

9. How do I recover if the builder/developer is out of business, cannot be located or is bankrupt?

Homeowner associations and homeowners should carefully assess the developer's ability to pay damages. The most important asset in many states is the developer's insurance. Even if the developer cannot be located or is bankrupt, the insurance companies must defend and pay claims that are covered under the policy(ies). Determine early on how much insurance the developer maintained from completion of construction to the present and how much is left. Eastern states have limited developer insurance. It is critical to evaluate the assets not only of the builder but of the general contractor, subcontractors, architect and engineer, as well.

10. Will the owners or homeowner association's insurance company cover damages caused by construction defects?

No. The language in most owner and homeowner association insurance policies has dramatically changed over the last decade. Insurance companies have now rewritten their policies to exclude most of the types of coverage that previously provided benefits for construction defects. Disaster coverage (flood, earthquake, and hurricane) must be separately evaluated.

11. Am I required to make repairs while the lawsuit is pending, and can I recover those costs in the lawsuit?

Yes and yes. You are required to take all reasonable steps to protect the property from sustaining additional damage. These costs are normally recoverable in the lawsuit. Carefully review any temporary repair program with an expert to guarantee correct documentation of the repairs. If you can delay some of the temporary repairs until permanent repairs can be made without causing additional damage to the property, a great deal of money may be saved.

12. Can I sell or refinance my home during the litigation?

Yes. The board of directors has a fiduciary duty to investigate homeowner complaints of common area construction defects and timely pursue a claim against the developer to recover damages and fix the problems. During this time, a homeowner must disclose to a potential buyer common area defects and litigation. Such disclosure may have an impact on sales. Consult a real estate broker who is experienced in working with homes in litigation. Due to fluctuating interest rates, many owners may want to refinance their homes. While in litigation, lenders are cautious about refinancing. Consult with an experienced mortgage broker. There are several mortgage companies that specialize in refinancing homes involved in litigation.

APPENDIX D:
ELEVEN BUILDERS' MYTHS

"TRUST ME . . . I'M THE BUILDER" OR
ELEVEN DECONSTRUCTED BUILDERS' MYTHS

1. BUILDERS' COMMENT:

"This is not a defect. It's a normal crack. Stucco and concrete slabs always crack, windows and doors always leak. It's typical as a house settles in."

OUR RESPONSE: Don't believe it. While hairline cracks may occur, these cracks can and often do increase in size with time and represent poorly compacted or expansive soils that expand and contract, structural problems, or poor construction practices. Also, windows and roofs should never leak. If any of these things occur, photograph them over time and watch how they change in size and character.

2. BUILDERS' COMMENT:

"Don't worry, I've fixed your problems."

OUR RESPONSE: Builders, their customer service staff, and repair contractors rarely fix the underlying problem. They will patch, plug, paint over cracks and caulk just about anything. Before you know it, your time to file an action has lapsed. Builders will never **replace** and will never tell you what's really causing the roof to leak, plumbing to fail or electrical fixtures to flicker. Only "Band Aid" or cosmetic repairs are made, time and time again.

3. BUILDERS' COMMENT:

"Your one year warranty is up, you're out of time."

OUR RESPONSE: The typical builder warranty is but one very small measure of a homeowner's protection. Owners have several years after home completion (between four and ten, depending on the jurisdiction) to seek damages for defects. Don't be misled.

4. BUILDERS' COMMENT:

"You have an extended 10-year warranty backed by insurance that will cover all workmanship or material defects in your home."

OUR RESPONSE: Hogwash. These written warranties are often **not** worth the paper they're written on. Most of these warranties are nothing more than a sophisticated marketing scheme intended to sell you a new home. These policies rarely provide protection for any significant defects. Read the fine print. How it defines a defect follows no respected industry standards.

5. BUILDERS' COMMENT:

"You have no claim because your city building inspectors have signed off on your home as meeting all building codes."

OUR RESPONSE: Building inspectors never have the time to inspect every home in your development to see if they meet all building codes. Most only have time to do cursory inspections. Don't be fooled. It is no defense that the building inspection department has signed off on your home.

6. BUILDERS' COMMENT:

"Your property will be tied up for four or five years in a lawsuit."

OUR RESPONSE: Ninety percent of lawsuits are resolved within 24 months of filing, and of those, ninety percent will settle and never go to trial. Most attorneys will work on a contingency fee basis. They get paid when they win. They are motivated to expedite a settlement.

7. BUILDERS' COMMENT:

"If you file a lawsuit, you will have to disclose that you have defects and the value of your house or condo will suffer."

OUR RESPONSE: Don't panic. Building defects are common. Savvy real estate agents know how to deal with disclosures and financing if you have to sell before the case is resolved. It is the defects in your home that must be disclosed. But the builder, not you, caused the problem. The sooner you file, the quicker the settlement and the faster you receive money to fix the defects. Once the lawsuit is dismissed, the stigma quickly diminishes, and your duty to disclose only continues if you don't fix the problems.

8. BUILDERS' COMMENT:

"You'll never get a dime from me, I'm out of business (or went into bankruptcy) and my corporation was only a shell with no assets."

OUR RESPONSE: All builders have liability insurance and most require their subcontractors to obtain additional insurance if a builder is sued for construction defects. Whether the builder is solvent, bankrupt or out of business, all insurance available when the defects appear will cover the builder and defend any lawsuit.

9. BUILDERS' COMMENT:

"You don't have to hire an independent expert. We're the experts—we built your home. We know what's wrong with it and we'll fix it."

OUR RESPONSE: Why would you trust the person who caused the problem in the first place to come back and fix it right? Without someone independent of the builder to first investigate the cause of the problem and provide a *proper* fix, you'll never know if the repair is permanent. Many construction defect law firms can arrange independent inspections free of charge.

10. BUILDERS' COMMENT:

"Construction defect lawyers go around soliciting homeowners and board members and trump up frivolous claims."

OUR RESPONSE: Nonsense. Over one-third of all production houses have significant construction defects. Board members of homeowner associations have a duty to investigate owner complaints, and if real, to take appropriate action. Homeowners can do what they want and have no obligation, but are foolish if they let the builder off the hook. Insurance companies for builders continue to pay out millions of dollars annually to fix builders' mistakes.

11. BUILDERS' COMMENT:

"Don't even think you will win is you sue us for defects, we will bury you."

OUR RESPONSE: Experienced construction defect attorneys will take your case on contingency, advance significant expert costs, and take the risk if you lose. Many are as well financed to hold their own and more with any developer or their insurance companies.

APPENDIX E: TOP 15 REASONS WHY BUILDERS FACE CONSTRUCTION DEFECT LAWSUITS

1. Poor customer service.
2. Inadequate architectural plans and details.
3. Lack of proper supervision.
4. Lowest bid/unqualified subcontract laborers.
5. Failing to address BOD defect claims by calling them HOA maintenance responsibilities.
6. Conflict of interest claims of HOA developer-controlled board.
7. Overstating builder qualifications—puffing.
8. Overstating quality home amenities—promising too much.
9. Failure to meet homeowner one-year warranty expectations.
10. Not providing clubhouse, pools, or other common area amenities.
10. Absence of homeowner maintenance manuals.
11. Poor developer transition.
13. Poor site selection—geology.
14. Building boom phenomenon—onto the next project.
15. Setting reserves too low.

For more information, see our website at www.constructiondefects.com, give us a call at 1-800-403-3332, or fax us at 1-800-323-0607.

HOME AND CONDO DEFECTS:
ORDER FORM

Name: _____

Address: _____

City: _____

State: _____

Zip:

E-mail: _____

Daytime phone: _____

Type of development: Home _____ Condo _____

Name of development: _____

Would you like a free inspection? Yes _____ No _____

Would you like more information about The Miller Law Firm?

    Yes _____ No _____

Would you like additional copies of this guide? Yes _____ No _____

The Miller Law Firm
4685 MacArthur Court, Suite 300
Newport Beach, CA 92660
(800) 403-3332
www.constructiondefects.com